SITTING BULL SPEAKS

The Life and Times of the Lakota Sioux Leader

SITTING BULL SPEAKS

The Life and Times of the Lakota Sioux Leader

Edited, with an Introduction,
by Brad D. Lookingbill

H | Hackett Publishing Company
    Indianapolis

Copyright © 2025 by Hackett Publishing Company, Inc.

All rights reserved
Printed in the United States of America

28 27 26 25   1 2 3 4 5 6 7

For further information, please address
Hackett Publishing Company, Inc.
P.O. Box 44937
Indianapolis, Indiana 46244-0937

www.hackettpublishing.com

Cover and interior design by E. L. Wilson
Composition by Aptara, Inc.

Cataloging-in-Publication data can be accessed via the Library of Congress Online Catalog. Library of Congress Control Number: 2025935670

ISBN-13: 978-1-64792-240-5 (pbk.)
ISBN-13: 978-1-64792-245-0 (PDF ebook)
ISBN-13: 978-1-64792-246-7 (epub)

The paper used in this publication meets the minimum requirements of American National Standard for Information Sciences—Permanence of Paper for Printed Library Materials, ANSI Z39.48–1984.

∞

Contents

Acknowledgments	*vii*
List of Illustrations	*viii*
Chronology	*ix*
Introduction: A Lakota Life	1
Note on Sources and Methods	35
Part 1: Emergence	39
Part 2: Battleground	63
Part 3: Border Crossings	89
Part 4: Standing Rock	119
Postscript: Something Said in Passing	149
Endnotes	*155*
Questions for Discussion	*169*
Glossary	*171*
Selected Bibliography	*175*
Image Credits	*185*
Index	*187*

ACKNOWLEDGMENTS

I wish to thank many individuals who helped to bring this book to fruition. I am fortunate to work at Columbia College of Missouri, where the administration provided a summer grant and a one-semester sabbatical. The chair of the Humanities Department, David Karr, authorized funds for book acquisitions and conference attendance. I appreciate the support of colleagues and students, who encouraged me to think through primary sources. Members of the library staff, especially Mary Batterson, Vandy Evermon, and Peter Neely, tracked down important materials. I am indebted to the University of Oklahoma's Western History Collections, the Smithsonian Institution's National Anthropological Archives, the Library of Congress, and the National Archives and Records Administration. Gary Clayton Anderson, an outstanding scholar at the University of Oklahoma, introduced me to the "paradox of Lakota nationhood" almost three decades ago. During the COVID-19 pandemic, Jeffrey D. Means, an enrolled member of the Oglala Sioux Tribe and a historian at the University of Wyoming, met with me through Zoom. The anonymous readers of the manuscript itself offered helpful suggestions for improvement. Liz Wilson of Hackett Publishing managed the production process with care. It has been my privilege to collaborate with Rick Todhunter, senior editor at Hackett Publishing, who recognized the value of this book for classrooms.

I owe a special thanks to my wife, Deidra, for her assistance in all things great and small. As my son, Augustus, and my daughter, Beatrice, can attest, she keeps our world turning. I dedicate this book to her. All mistakes remain mine alone.

List of Illustrations

1. Winter Count, twentieth century, Lakȟóta.
2. Map, Treaty of Fort Laramie, 1851.
3. Map, Treaty of Fort Laramie, 1868.
4. Custer's War, c. 1900, Tȟatȟáŋka Waŋžíla (Henry Oscar One Bull).
5. Front Page, *Harper's Weekly*, December 8, 1877.
6. Sitting Bull, half-length portrait, seated, facing front, holding calumet, 1881.
7. Sitting Bull and Buffalo Bill.
8. Map, Lakota Reservations, 1890.
9. "Let us put our minds together and see what life we will make for our children."
10. A drawing of war deeds of Sitting Bull and Jumping Bull.
11. In battle with Flatheads.
12. A Map Partly Suggested and Corrected by Chief Sitting Bull.
13. In battle with Crow scouts accompanying General Nelson A. Miles.
14. Photograph of Buffalo Robe Painting by Sitting Bull.
15. US commissioners and delegations of Sioux chiefs visiting Washington, October 13, 1888.

Chronology

1803	The United States purchases the Louisiana Territory from France
1804	The Corps of Discovery encounters the Lakota Sioux
1812	The War of 1812
1823	Arikara War
1831	Sitting Bull born
1833	Leonid meteor shower
1837–1840	Smallpox epidemic on the Great Plains
1846–1848	The Mexican-American War
1851	First Fort Laramie Treaty
1854	The Grattan Fight
1857	First comprehensive map of the Trans-Mississippi West
1861	Dakota Territory established
1862	Dakota War in Minnesota
1865	The US Civil War ends at Appomattox Court House
1866–1868	Red Cloud's War
1868	Second Fort Laramie Treaty
1869	First Transcontinental Railroad
1871	Indian Appropriations Act
1873	Panic of 1873
1874	Military expedition finds gold in the Black Hills
1876	The Great Sioux War
1877	The Agreement of 1877
	Sitting Bull camps in the Dominion of Canada
	Crazy Horse killed
1878	The Great Dakota Boom begins
1881	Sitting Bull detained by the US Army

1883	Sitting Bull assigned to Standing Rock
1884	The Sitting Bull Combination debuts
1885	Sitting Bull travels with Buffalo Bill's Wild West show
1887	Dawes Act
1889	The Sioux Agreement
	North Dakota and South Dakota statehood
	The Ghost Dance spreads
1890	Sitting Bull killed
	Wounded Knee Massacre
1893	Sitting Bull's cabin exhibited at the World's Fair
1924	Indian Citizenship Act
1953	Sitting Bull's bones relocated
1980	*United States v. Sioux Nation of Indians*

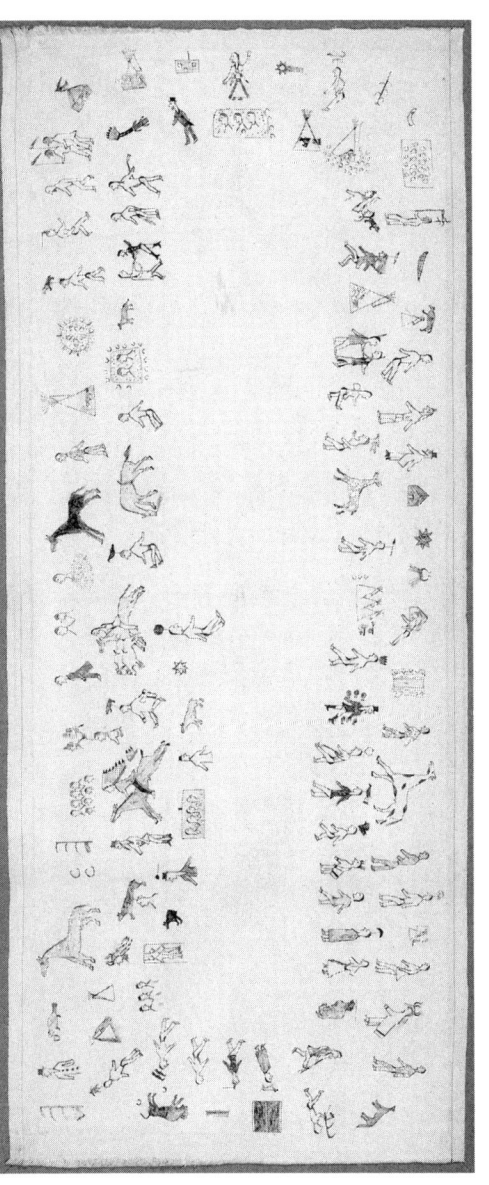

Winter Count, twentieth century, Lakȟóta.

INTRODUCTION:

A LAKOTA LIFE

Tatáŋka Íyotake is a Siouxan expression describing a male bison seated upon the prairie while watching over a herd. It translates into the phrase, "Buffalo Bull Who Sits," invoking a force of nature. A number of virtuous attributes—bravery, fortitude, generosity, and wisdom—are suggested by this phrase. The expression also was given as a name to a Lakota Sioux who devoted his life to protecting his people. He became known around the world by the Anglicized name Sitting Bull.[1]

A long time ago, Sitting Bull's ancestors began to occupy the land near the upper Missouri River in North America. Tribal historians preserved an oral tradition to recollect significant occurrences from age to age, as the Indigenous populations generated winter counts for memorialization. The winter count, a kind of pictographic record or calendar, highlighted a major event of a single year, arranging imagery in configurations on animal hides. The first events depicted in the traditional Lakota Sioux winter counts relate to episodes during the late eighteenth century. Although the term "Sioux" eventually became a linguistic appellation that covers a related people amid a vast wilderness, it began as a French corruption of a central Algonquian word that once meant "snake." The name Lakota comes from an autonym for the "united" or "allied" western Sioux, who shared power, knowledge, and language. Also known by the name Teton, they were "dwellers on the prairie." They comprised seven tribal bands of distinct people, or oyátes: the Hunkpapa, Oglala, Sicangu [Brulé], Sihasapa [Blackfoot], Miniconjou, Two Kettle, and Sans Arc. Even if they spoke variant Siouxan dialects, they shared a sense of geopolitical identity through the Očhéthi Šakówiŋ, or Seven Council Fires.[2]

The Lakota developed identifiable traits associated with the classic buffalo-hunting cultures of the North American Great Plains. A band of extended family groups ranging from 150 to 300 individuals, called tiospayes, or collection of lodges, camped together. Their councils selected an *itancan*, or chief. The traditional male societies assembled the *akicitas*, or warriors, who provided security around campsites and scouted ahead for promising locations for food, water, and shelter. These warriors carried bows and arrows with them almost everywhere they went. The warriors' strategic adaptation of horses and firearms enabled them to extend their foraging excursions toward the setting sun and to broaden a conflict zone to the banks of the Bighorn River. Pushing westward across contested grounds, they confronted Indigenous rivals such as the Kiowa, Omaha, Ponca, Otoe, Flathead, Pawnee, Shoshone, Crow, Hidatsa, Blackfeet, Assiniboine, Gros Ventre, Mandan, and Arikara. In 1823, they assisted the *wasi'chus*—non-Indian people of western European descent—by raiding Arikara villages along the upper Missouri. Their mobility was a tactical asset and made them less susceptible to the outbreaks of disease that decimated so many of the other Native Americans following the arrival of the *wasi'chus* on this continent. While organizing a suzerainty in their section, the nomadic folk saw little reason to fear the existence of the US government. By the middle of the nineteenth century, the Lakota population had grown to as many as fifteen thousand. As long as millions of bison roamed the inland steppes of the occupied territories, the vernacular space of the "Buffalo Nation" sustained grand communal hunts for game.[3]

Emergence

"I was born on the Missouri River," stated Sitting Bull to a journalist later in life, although the exact location and precise date of his birth remain indefinite.[4] Most biographers point to 1831, which slightly predates a magnificent meteor shower that indexed multiple Lakota winter counts. His father bore the name Sitting Bull at the time of his birth, and he was given the name Jumping Badger. His mother, Her Holy Door, raised him in a tipi along with his three sisters—one older named Good Feather Woman and two younger named Twin Woman and Brown Shawl Woman. The beloved child survived a bout with smallpox, which left minor scarring on his face. Steadfast, vigilant, and deliberate, he acquired the nickname *Hunkesni*, which meant Slow. His boyhood talents included an uncanny ability to listen attentively to the sounds of animals, especially birds. As both a participant and an observer, he enjoyed the songs, dances, and artistry common to the *hochoka*, or camp circle. Educated by two uncles, Four Horns and Looks-for-Him-in-a-Tent, he was considered a gifted athlete. He strove to excel at footraces. He also earned applause in a popular hoop game, a team sport involving sticks used for the purpose of rolling objects across an open field. His teachers demanded long hours on horseback to develop the martial skills necessary for navigating the prairies. His peers called him Sacred Standshot. He demonstrated exceptional prowess with the bow and arrow, killing his first buffalo by the time he was ten years old.[5]

As preparation for the responsibilities of adulthood, the *hanblecheyapi*, or vision quest, was a pivotal event in the life of a Lakota youth. With the aid of a spiritual advisor, a young man would retire, alone, to some quiet spot away from the lodges to endure fasting, meditation, and sleeplessness. Only the worthy would experience a revelatory dream. The dreaming state liberated the imagination from ordinary space and time, eliminating the perceptual boundaries between the visible and invisible worlds. If a divine spirit revealed itself during the brief seclusion, it would become an invaluable guide on the road of life. A neophyte experienced the "crying for a vision" as a rite of passage, although a vision's meaning was highly subjective, representing a confidential matter between an individual and his advisor. As a teenager, Jumping Badger dreamed about marvelous birds watching over him from trees and hilltops. Later, painting his face with lightning, he may have sensed the spiritual calling of a *heyoka*—a strange and wondrous human being summoned to a glorious purpose by the thunderbird, a mythological winged creature. A thunderbird dreamer belonged to an exclusive fraternity, whose actions seemed inexplicable to the uninitiated observer. They were foremost among a camp's guardians and known for their fearlessness in the face of danger. They protected friends and family from emerging threats and prepared to sacrifice themselves in battle without a second thought.[6]

The elder Sitting Bull's only son experienced his first battle around the age of fourteen. He bravely counted his first coup, which was a warrior's way of winning prestige by striking or touching an enemy during combat. After earning a white feather during a furious fight with the Crow

Indians, he received the name Sitting Bull as a gift from his proud father, who thereafter became known as Jumping Bull. His father also gave him a sacred shield decorated with a dark birdlike creature in the center of a blue-green field. He also received a long lance with an eight-inch notched iron blade. After a subsequent clash with the Flathead Indians, he earned a red feather for suffering his first wound. A second wound, received during another skirmish with the Crow, caused a limp that remained apparent as he matured. He was initiated into the Strong Hearts, Kit Fox, and Buffalo societies, which conferred their exclusive honors upon the most respected.[7]

Though the Hunkpapa band shaped his daily life, little is known about the personal affairs of the young Sitting Bull. His first wife, Light Hair, whom he married in 1851, died in 1857. His first son died a short time later. He married at least two additional wives, Scarlet Woman and Snow on Hair. Consequently, he shared his lodge with as many as nine different wives over the course of his adult years. He parented a number of biological children, including two daughters, Many Horses and Standing Holy, and a son, Crow Foot. He raised a nephew, One Bull, much as a son, assuming responsibility for his instruction just as Four Horns and Looks-for-Him-in-a-Tent had educated him. Another nephew, White Bull, grew close to him on the warpath. He sustained an abiding friendship with his cousin Black Moon. Sitting Bull's father died in 1859 as the result of a stab wound received during an intertribal battle. Sitting Bull's adopted brother *Hohe*, originally called Little Assiniboine, then took the name Jumping Bull. Sitting Bull's widowed mother remained a guiding light around the tipi, staying within his inner circle until her death in 1884.[8]

Standing five feet, ten inches in height, Sitting Bull rose to prominence in the Lakota's cultural world. He possessed a muscular frame, broad shoulders, and long hair, but it was his reputation for "making medicine" that inspired many to follow him. His dark brown eyes observed what could not be seen in the uncertainties of the wide, open spaces. With a spiritual mindset, he endeavored to solve chronic problems such as insecurity, sickness, thirst, and hunger. His understanding of an interconnected cosmos imparted knowledge and power through constant communication with *Wakantanka*—the Great Mysterious One or the Great Spirit. He believed that an all-embracing, life-giving energy strengthened every form of existence, and he sensed its manifestations in the sky, wind, rain, rocks,

Introduction: A Lakota Life 5

streams, and trees. He focused his intellect on the sacred gifts of a paternal Sun and a maternal Earth. He recognized the vital importance of the bison ecology, which offered meat for food, hides for clothing and shelter, and countless items for daily use. His vocabulary suggested equivalencies with religious orthodoxies and articulated an appreciation of the incomprehensible forces that made him a *wichásha wakán*, or holy man. He carried a *wotawe*, a medicine bundle containing a small white stone, human hair rolled into little balls, and bits of wood and shell. He became well-known for his charms, prophecies, and prayerfulness. Undoubtedly, he embodied the four cardinal virtues of the Lakota: bravery, fortitude, generosity, and wisdom. "I was never afraid of my enemies," he declared, for "my successes I owe the Great Spirit."⁹

Sitting Bull played a conspicuous role in the *wiwáŋyaŋg wachipi*, or sun dances, annual outpourings of spiritual devotion among the Lakota. The otherwise independent *oyátes* prepared each year for the communal hunts by fulfilling personal vows of ceremonial self-sacrifice. With the scattered bands coming together in summer, the *wiwáŋyaŋg wachipi* rekindled a collaborative ethos with festivities, feasting, and frolics. The dances lasted up to six days and were held in an outdoor arena. For a *wichásha wakán*, these rituals typically involved pantomiming, fasting, meditating, and gazing upward at the blazing orb in the sky. Inserting skewers through their skin, the participants moved around a "medicine pole" and strained to break free. The scars on Sitting Bull's chest, back, and arms testified of the physical pain while sun dancing.¹⁰

One of the most important touchstones of Sitting Bull's belief system was the sacredness of the *Pahá Sápa*, or Black Hills. This singular, isolated mountain range loomed large on the horizon with rugged granite spires crowning its peaks. It towered some four thousand feet skyward over prairie grasses, pine trees, and spring-fed waters. It encompassed an area over a hundred miles long and almost fifty miles wide. Its ridges, curves, and recesses evoked the form of a reclining female body, or so hunters and gatherers observed. It was said that the first buffalo emerged from a cavern, which opened at the base of the *Pahá Sápa. Iktomi*, a spider-trickster spirit and shape-shifting hero of Lakota folklore, purportedly invited the original human beings to follow the buffalo's passageway to the mountain meadows. To Sitting Bull and his people, the Black Hills became a site of

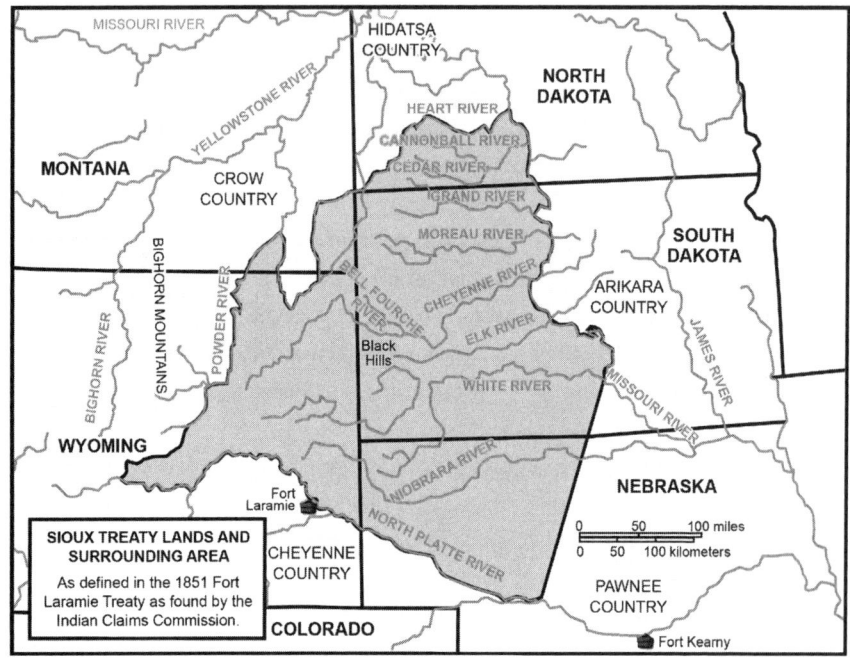

Map, Treaty of Fort Laramie, 1851.

transcendence, representing the heart of everything that sustains life on the northern Great Plains.[11]

Preferring to remain close to the Black Hills, Sitting Bull stayed away from the remote military outposts being built by the *wasi'chus*. He ignored the treaty council held between Plains Indians and governmental authorities near Fort Laramie, which granted the United States permission to build roads and forts in the interior borderlands. Also called the Horse Creek Treaty, this first Fort Laramie Treaty was signed on September 17, 1851. Though the US government recognized tribal territorial claims, Sitting Bull considered the treaty's provisions irrelevant. Following the Dakota War of 1862 in Minnesota, he noticed Siouxan refugees relocating westward. At his northernmost camps, lodged along the upper Missouri—where some Lakota traded furs with the Chouteau Company at Fort Pierre—he encountered US soldiers on maneuvers around Fort Berthold. On July 28, 1864, he fought against the bluecoats in the Battle of Killdeer Mountain. He frustrated opponents in skirmishes at Dead Buffalo Lake and in the Badlands.

Introduction: A Lakota Life 7

Multiple war parties annoyed the "soldier houses" of Fort Stevenson, Fort Totten, Fort Rice, and Fort Buford, even if he avoided set-piece actions. The "Long Knives"—non-Indian invaders—did not fight like traditional enemies, he observed, but campaigned in massive formations across contested ground and utilized the firepower of field artillery known as "thunder iron." Of course, he preferred hit-and-run tactics. When a Hunkpapa village held a non-Indian female named Fanny Kelly, seized during an Oglala raid, Sitting Bull insisted that she be returned safely to Fort Sully. He received another wound in battle when a ball from a revolver struck him in the left hip and exited out the small of his back. He healed quickly, even as his widowed mother counseled him against taking too many risks.[12]

In light of all this, it is perhaps unsurprising that Sitting Bull's reputation for acts of valor began to spread far and wide. One Lakota winter count identifies the "first fight with white men," depicting him battling a US soldier between 1864 and 1865. Generally unconcerned with the US Civil War, Plains Indians tended to focus their attention on military outfits around the "Great American Desert." A few glyphs feature flags that commemorate formal conferences with US commissioners, although Sitting Bull boasted that he never signed any accords with those "taking lands."[13]

Signed by Lakota representatives and US commissioners on July 2, 1868, the second Fort Laramie Treaty ended the belligerence of Red Cloud, an Oglala Lakota chief. While arranging peace "between the parties to this agreement," this treaty established the Great Sioux Reservation in the Dakota Territory. The 48,000 square miles encompassed the White, Bad, Cheyenne, Moreau, and Grand Rivers as well as the Black Hills. Granting the Lakota a substantial realm that extended about two hundred miles from south to north, the treaty secured for them "absolute and undisturbed use and occupation" of the land. Vague references to railroad rights-of-way left the door open for future infrastructure projects but did not explain the devilish details. The treaty closed the Bozeman Trail, an overland route in the Montana Territory, and military outposts were abandoned. The legalisms of the treaty's seventeen articles placed constraints upon the Lakota, or so officials in Washington DC assumed. Nevertheless, Article 11 recognized hunting rights for the Lakota as far south as the Republican River. Its language reserved the right to "hunt on any lands north of the North Platte River and on the Republican Fork of the Smoky Hill River," so long as the bison herds ranged thereon "in such

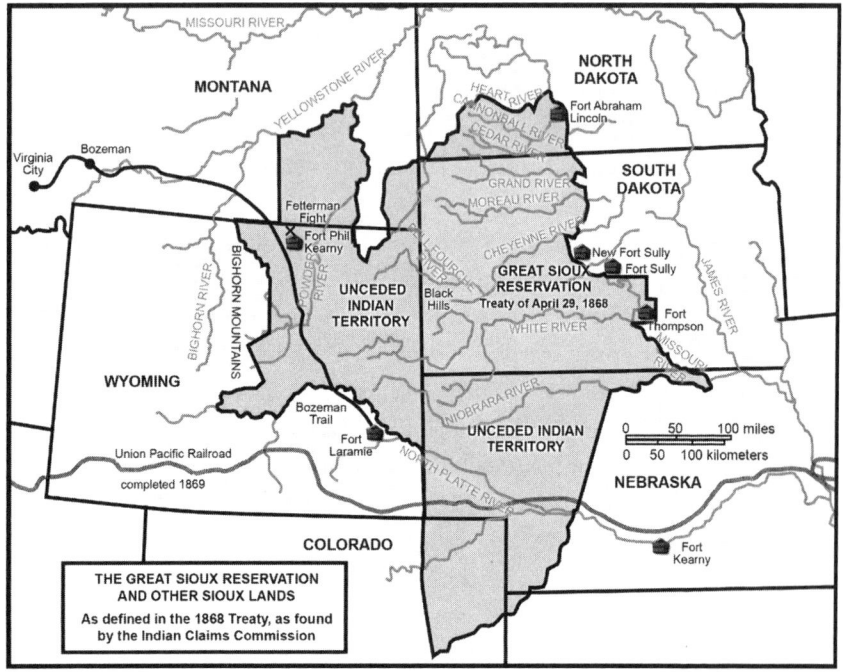

Map, Treaty of Fort Laramie, 1868.

numbers as to justify the chase." According to Article 16, the lands north of the North Platte River and eastward from the summits of the Big Horn Mountains remained "unceded Indian territory." Henceforth, "no white person or persons" would be permitted to settle upon or to occupy any portion of it without Lakota approval. The US government promised financial payments to the Lakota for the building of potential roads and pledged that no future agreement for land cessions would be considered valid unless executed and signed by "at least three-fourths of the adult male Indians."[14]

As the Lakota carried out vendettas against the Crow Indians and other rivals, US citizens boosted plans for the development of transcontinental railroads across the country. In 1868, Ulysses S. Grant, a former US Army officer known for his successful campaigns in the Civil War, won the presidential election and took office in Washington DC the following year. He openly courted the public service of humanitarian reformers, who decried the wars of Indian extermination and extolled the morality of the "white man's road." Despite the stated purpose of bureaucratic initiatives, defending Indian rights remained secondary to economic interests. Non-Indian homesteaders, ranchers, and miners pushed further and further westward even as tribal groups supposedly held the "reserved" lands, usually defined by shifting boundaries as established in a plethora of treaties with congressional approval. Leaders such as Red Cloud made numerous trips to and from the national capital, urging governmental authorities to fulfill their obligations. Obviously, the reservation system—and the reduction of freedom under it—was not what the Indigenous populations of the North American grasslands wanted. Throughout the Reconstruction era, the "peace policy" of the Grant administration would lead to sharp wars between US soldiers and the Plains Indians.[15]

Meanwhile, Sitting Bull acted as a *blotáhunka*, or war chief, guarding the Lakota's terrain. By the end of the 1860s, he had counted sixty-three coups in martial feats that bested foes. His calm temperament diffused tensions at tribal councils, for he often sat quietly, rehearsing in his mind what he would say or do before proceeding. His uncompromising repudiation of the *wasi'chus* resonated with the belligerent voices, who wanted to hunt without external constraints and desired to avoid dependency on the US government. His uncle Four Horns, a ranking Hunkpapa chieftain, encouraged Sitting Bull to seek an innovative leadership position in an era of political instability. "When you tell us to fight, we will raise up our weapons," proclaimed the Shirt Wearer to Sitting Bull, "and if you tell us to make peace, we will lay down our weapons." The elevation of Sitting Bull to higher authority may have been temporary, for it depended on the willingness of non-treaty factions to abide by their pledges of loyalty. In a grand ceremony, he was carried into a large circle on a buffalo robe and crowned with a magnificent headdress. An enthusiastic crowd applauded the anointment of a *wakicunza*, or honored administrator, who sought to unite the separate clans and diverse bands for action. There was no precedent for this kind of senior executive role, which exalted unity of command. Sitting Bull's supporters heralded him as the "Supreme Chief of the whole Sioux Nation," even if this was an exaggeration. His critics considered him a great pretender since he was not a hereditary figurehead. Though not supported by everyone, he exerted broader influence than had any other Lakota before him.[16]

Battleground

The bison herds drew many Lakota to the far western stretches of the upper Missouri, where Sitting Bull solidified his leadership during the early 1870s. He remained an advocate for self-sufficiency on the northern Great Plains, and his camp attracted a wide following from the discontented souls seeking both sustenance and security. For example, he befriended Frank Grouard, a former captive with mixed Polynesian ancestry. Intertribal warfare remained a popular pastime, and another wounding earned him an additional red feather. His raids even targeted caravans of roving Canadian Métis traders, often denigrated as the Slota, or "greasy ones," who crisscrossed the interior borderlands to exchange rifles and ammunition for buffalo hides. Always camping a safe distance from the columns of US soldiers, he recognized that the changes in the land made it difficult to get "something to eat." He sent His Horse Looking, the husband of a younger sister, to Fort Peck, instructing his brother-in-law to seek out "a white man who would tell the truth" and promising to visit if one could be found. He would not commit to going to Washington DC and avoided meeting with the temporizing envoys of the "Great Father," or the US president. His camp accepted rations for the first time but continued to depend on foraging. Whether or not peace was attainable, he wanted to make the Powder River country into a game reserve for the Lakota.[17]

Events along the Yellowstone River, which the Lakota called the Elk River, attracted the attention of Sitting Bull. He observed the disruptive activities of the "rail road people" in 1872 and sent word through an emissary to Colonel David S. Stanley that any invasion of the hunting grounds would be met by force. He consulted the Silent Eaters, a secret group amid the Strong Hearts that gathered at midnight to achieve consensus for strategic planning and tactical coordination. He mobilized a cadre of equestrians known as the White Horse Riders, who came to be called "Sitting Bull's soldiers." In the valley of the Yellowstone, surveyor teams and military escorts for the Northern Pacific Railway endured a concerted strike led by Sitting Bull himself. A stunning display of his audacity occurred on August 14, 1872, when the Lakota tangled with Major Eugene M. Baker's command in the Battle of Arrow Creek. In the midst of a gunfire exchange, Sitting Bull strolled down range and sat on the ground in front of the bluecoats. Inviting comrades to join him in the danger zone, he proceeded to enjoy a leisurely smoke of tobacco in the range of sharpshooters—all the while ignoring the hail of bullets whizzing by his head. After puffing on his pipe, he cleaned it and then walked off the line, unfazed by the chaos around him. White Bull, his nephew and fellow smoker, called it "the bravest deed possible." Once the construction of the Northern Pacific Railway foundered, the financial empire of Jay Cooke and Company collapsed in bankruptcy a year later.[18]

As a result of sensational press releases from the US Army's Expedition of 1874, close to fifteen thousand migrants swarmed the Black Hills to search for gold. The next year, Sitting Bull vowed to defend what he called the Lakota "food pack"—the Black Hills—from the trespassers. His supporters tried to shut down the "thieves' road," a trail that cut through the Great Sioux Reservation. To intimidate gold-diggers in their midst, mounted Indian warriors took to yelling, "Sitting Bull, I am he!" President Grant, who contemplated ways to "extinguish Indian title" to the mineral resources in the Black Hills, huddled with the military brass and deskbound bureaucrats in the White House. Following the Indian Appropriations Act of 1871, the legislative branch prohibited new treaties with tribal groups. While the rations and annuities from the agencies were placed on hold, officials in Washington DC no longer abided by the Fort Laramie Treaty. They demanded that the Lakota sell the Black Hills, cease camping off the reservation, and prepare to relocate to Indian Territory within the southern Great Plains. The US government and its surrogates announced that any cohorts not residing within reservation boundaries by January 31, 1876, would be considered "hostile."[19]

After receiving reports of depredations committed by the Plains Indians, the War Department prepared the armed forces for imminent hostilities. Lieutenant General Philip H. Sheridan, commander of the Military Division of the Missouri, formulated a plan to use three converging columns to drive the roaming bands into confinement. One column, led by Brigadier General George Crook, moved northward from Fort Fetterman in present-day Wyoming. Under Colonel John Gibbon, another column headed eastward from western Montana. The third column, commanded by Brigadier General Alfred H. Terry, marched westward from Fort Abraham Lincoln in the Dakota Territory. Surrounded on all sides, Lakota families living off the reservation had nowhere to turn without facing US soldiers. General Sheridan anticipated a quick victory during the centennial campaign, but logistical problems postponed most of the overland movements until the spring and summer months.²⁰

Thus began the Great Sioux War of 1876, which General Sheridan once called "Sitting Bull's War."²¹ The lethality of Sitting Bull was renowned all over the countryside, where tribal groups attempted to organize a wartime coalition against the United States. Sitting Bull sent messengers to the circles of camps scattered up and down the Missouri, asking kinsmen to join him in the hunting grounds. As men, women, and children abandoned the agencies and sought their sustenance near the Powder River, his encampment offered food, water, and shelter to many that spring. From May 21 to May 24, he communed with the Great Spirit from the heights of a butte along Rosebud Creek. After meditating atop a moss-covered rock, he experienced a "terrible dream" about a dust storm propelled by a threatening gale from the east. He envisioned uniformed invaders advancing overland, their weaponry, accoutrements, and trimmings visible in the sunlight. When the approaching tempest crashed into a white cloud, thunder rolled, lightning cracked, and rains poured. Nothing was left of the dust storm; the threat disappeared from sight. The front drifted serenely to the east and to the north. Thereafter, the clear skies indicated to Sitting Bull that the Plains Indians would survive the onslaught from the US Army. "If you do this for me," Sitting Bull pleaded to *Wakantanka* on the multitude's behalf, "I will sun dance two days and nights and will give you a whole buffalo."²²

In the Montana Territory, thousands of brave companions joined Sitting Bull for a sun dance below the mouth of Muddy Creek. Following purification in a sweat lodge on June 6, he entered the dance circle and performed a pipe ceremony. His associates cut his arms at least a hundred times, gouging tiny pieces of flesh from his body. He danced around the "medicine pole," staring intently into the blazing orb overhead. After half an hour, as blood oozed from the gashes on his skin, he received a new vision. Looking upward with highly attuned senses, he saw bluecoats, as "numerous as grasshoppers" on horseback, riding upside down as they descended on a Plains Indian village. With their feet pointing to the heavens, the soldiers' hats fell toward the Earth. A chilling voice from beyond proclaimed: "These soldiers do not possess ears. They are to die, but you are not supposed to take their spoils." Sitting Bull, who heard the warning loud and clear, readied the campers for a major battle in the offing.²³

Lakota, Cheyenne, and Arapaho communities—as many as seven thousand people—took sanctuary in the valley of the Little Bighorn River, although they called the area the Greasy Grass. Their sense of solidarity brought a determination to confront the three converging columns of the US Army. On June 17, their war parties stymied General Crook's column in the Battle of the Rosebud, forcing the regiments to return to a base camp at the Tongue River. At the behest of General Terry, Lieutenant Colonel George Armstrong Custer of the Seventh Cavalry located the Little Bighorn lodges with the assistance of Crow and Arikara scouts. On June 25, Custer, a well-known Civil War veteran casually nicknamed "Long Hair" by the Plains Indians, maneuvered into an attack position above the encampment. With the sounds of war cries in the air, his reconnaissance in force turned into a bloody disaster. He died near a hilltop, where Sitting Bull earlier had honored the Great Spirit with an offering of a buffalo robe and tobacco bundles. The non-Indians called this encounter "Custer's Last Stand." Elsewhere along the ridgeline, a handful of shattered US companies survived on a high bluff. Outnumbered more than three to one, 268 men with Custer's detachment died in the clash. The combined losses among the Plains Indians numbered far less with perhaps thirty-one killed in action. In what came to be known as the Battle of the Little Bighorn, the US Army suffered its worst defeat of the Plains Indian wars.[24]

Amid the dust and noise in the Little Bighorn valley, Sitting Bull exited the battlefield within hours. The women, children, and elderly of the encampment needed his help, and he saved these noncombatants by leading them farther west into the Big Horn Mountains. Still recovering from the sun dance, he focused his energies on protecting the camp's most vulnerable from Custer's sudden attack. While pandemonium erupted, he gave commands to the defenders assembling from the flats to the ravines. "Brave up, boys," he repeated upon hearing the roar of gunfire, "it will be a hard time." The unsung heroes in combat were younger men, most of whom battled the Long Knives in cohesive teams. The personal example of Crazy Horse, an Oglala leader, inspired scores to enter the fray while shouting: "*Hóka hé!*"—"Let's go!" Gall, one of Sitting Bull's adopted younger brothers, led Hunkpapa charges along the banks of the river. White Bull, the son of Sitting Bull's sister, also distinguished himself. They fought with Winchester, Henry, and Spencer repeating rifles as well as bows and arrows.

Their sweeping, circling maneuvers on horseback thwarted Custer's risky approach and overwhelmed the frantic men in uniform. Disadvantaged by their inferior numbers, the thin blue line fell apart under pressure. The victors departed the area on June 26, shortly before General Terry's reinforcements arrived.[25]

Ostensibly, Sitting Bull's insight into Custer's military objectives influenced his warrior's countermeasures. Though Sitting Bull never physically entered the fight, eyewitnesses saw him "sort of directing things" from the edge of the battlefield. He handed his sacred shield to One Bull, who carried it on his shoulder while riding his horse through the gun smoke. "Everything happened so quickly," Sitting Bull's nephew later recalled. Blood from a wounded comrade covered most of One Bull's body, but no bullet struck him during his daring ride. He returned to his uncle's side unharmed, observing firsthand that "the Indians and the soldiers were all lying mixed up all over the ground."[26] Although burial scaffolds and other markers adorned the bottomlands the day after, the sounds of wailing faded from the Greasy Grass.

America's telegraph offices and printing presses disseminated the breaking news of the "Custer Massacre," casting a pall over the centennial celebrations of 1876. The *New York Herald* referred to "the Napoleonic tactics and strategy of Sitting Bull." The *Chicago Daily Tribune* cited a Missouri steamboat captain, who claimed Sitting Bull was a Francophonic scholar of Napoleon Bonaparte. Noting the rumors spreading among military cadets, the *Baltimore Gazette* dubbed Sitting Bull "the Sioux West Pointer." A two-part forgery titled *The Works of Sitting Bull* included stanzas from contrived poetry in Greek, French, Spanish, English, Italian, German, and Latin. Published reports repeated falsehoods and hoaxes to rationalize the incredible turn of events.[27]

After learning of the stunning loss at the Little Bighorn, General Sheridan ordered 2,500 additional soldiers westward for a grand military march of retribution. "Custer's Avengers" deployed in heavy formations, as the rank and file prepared to deliver "stern punishment" to the nomadic folk unwilling to capitulate. US Army officers took command of the agencies and began dismounting, disarming, and detaining the Plains Indians. The US Congress disregarded the guarantees of the Fort Laramie Treaty, amending an appropriations bill to demand the formal cession of the Black

Introduction: A Lakota Life

Custer's War, c. 1900, Tȟatȟáŋka Waŋžíla (Henry Oscar One Bull).

Hills. Sitting Bull, however, refused to accept the outcome and confronted General Crook's command at Slim Buttes on September 9, 1876. To sustain military operations in these remote areas, the War Department authorized a cantonment at the junction of the Tongue and Yellowstone Rivers. On October 20, 1876, Colonel Nelson A. Miles, whom the Plains Indians called "Man with the Bear Coat," led the Fifth Infantry to Cedar Creek. Month after month Miles's well-supplied winter campaign made relentless progress, even when a blizzard engulfed the trails in every direction.[28] As the infantrymen marched across the windswept prairies, they would sing:

> We're marching off for Sitting Bull!
> And this is the way we go—
> Forty miles a day, on beans and hay,
> With the regular army, O![29]

As the wartime coalition of the Lakota, Cheyenne, and Arapaho unraveled, Sitting Bull recognized that the armed forces would eventually run him down. He scrambled along the Redwater River, a tributary of the upper Missouri, staying one step ahead of the pursuing columns. An intense engagement occurred at the Wolf Mountains on January 8, 1877, marking the last conventional battle of "Sitting Bull's War."[30]

Border Crossings

The United States organized a new commission to deliver an ultimatum to the Lakota Sioux: "Sell or starve." The Grant administration tapped George W. Manypenny, a former commissioner of Indian Affairs, to lead the drive to finalize an agreement with the agency headmen. The Great Father promised to provide rations and assistance until the Plains Indians became self-supporting. Perhaps unsurprisingly, no one bothered to obtain the number of legal signatures required under the Fort Laramie Treaty. On February 28, 1877, the US Congress officially ratified the agreement to take away the Black Hills and millions of acres from the Great Sioux Reservation.[31]

"We have two ways to go now," Sitting Bull announced to acolytes still following him, "to the land of the Grandmother (Canada) or to the land of the Spaniards (Mexico)."[32] Lakota war parties melted away, as desperate bands straggled into the agencies of the Dakota Territory. "Hang-Around-the-Fort" chiefs became hostages, held by the US Army officers in order to coerce their dependents into complying with federal mandates. On May 7, 1877, Crazy Horse and hundreds of fugitives surrendered at Camp Robinson in Nebraska. First held as a prisoner of war, the Oglala warrior was later killed, bayonetted in the back by guards during a scuffle. Elsewhere, military commands hired squads of Indian scouts to guide detachments through the Missouri bottoms. "Damn soldiers everywhere" became the Lakota lament on the run. While thousands of anxious souls resolved to cross the 49th parallel that marked the northern boundary of the United States, Sitting Bull tarried near the Big Bend of the Milk River. With the arrival of the warmer, longer days of spring, he eventually joined the exodus of refugees heading northward. They trekked along the *canku wakán*—a holy road—to seek sanctuary across the international border.[33]

Sitting Bull's wayfarers entered the "Grandmother's Land"—an allusion to the Dominion of Canada under British Queen Victoria. They journeyed along the White Mud River, but the loss of their ancestral homeland left many demoralized. Famine, illness, and grief stalked the makeshift lodgings of the exiles near Frenchman's Creek. The North-West Mounted Police, especially Major James M. Walsh, monitored the refugee camps on behalf of the territorial government. The influx of migrants prompted an exchange of diplomatic notes between Ottawa, London, and Washington DC. News spread that US President Rutherford B. Hayes and his cabinet conspired to arrange their shipment to Florida or to Indian Territory. At the direction of the Hayes administration, General Terry traveled north with US commissioners to offer pardons and amnesty to the holdouts. On October 17, 1877, a council was held in a large room at Fort Walsh. The angry Americans insisted that Sitting Bull must cease his "rambling mode of life," surrender all horses and weapons, become a cattle rancher, and live at an agency in the United States. He defiantly rejected their demands. One winter count calls this the "Year Sitting Bull Made Peace with the Englishman" and illustrates his hearty handshake with a friendly redcoat.[34]

Front Page, *Harper's Weekly*, December 8, 1877.

Though now a stranger in a strange place, Sitting Bull still lived free. He gazed upon the bison herds ranging near the grassy knolls of the Cypress Hills and the western flank of Wood Mountain. However, the game in the vicinity was insufficient to feed the roughly four thousand mouths in the refugee camps. The harsh weather exacerbated a mood of quiet desperation, yet the atmosphere in Canada remained congenial. "I am looking to the north for my life," Sitting Bull announced to Major Walsh in another council, for he expected the Mounties to keep the bluecoats at bay. Sitting Bull's campsite became a magnet for individuals often dismissed as "outlaws" fleeing the deplorable conditions of the reservation system. He welcomed a band of Nez Percé Indians, who eluded the US Army by crossing the international border. Colonel Miles chased one of Sitting Bull's hunting parties back to Fort Walsh, dispatching Crow auxiliaries to intercept them close to the Big Bend of the Milk River. Sitting Bull himself killed Magpie, a mounted Crow, in a dramatic duel on horseback. Despite Sitting Bull's association with incursions, Lakota animosity to the United States seemed to wane.[35]

On the southern side of the 49th parallel, the US government permitted the wholesale slaughter of the North American buffalo. Before the Great Sioux War millions of bison grazed the inland steppes; a decade later their numbers had plummeted to only a few thousand. Railways, soldiers, sportsmen, skinners, ranchers, homesteaders, and diseases dramatically reduced the herds, bringing the animals to the brink of extinction. The efficiency of new hunting technology and techniques increased the kill rates. Although the meat often rotted on the wasted carcasses of bison killed by the *wasi'chus*, the bones were ground into fertilizer for agricultural use. The mass shipment of Great Plains buffalo hides to industrial cities around the globe contributed to the terminal decline of a literal and figurative resource. The US Congress voted to appropriate funding for the first national park, Yellowstone, even if governmental efforts to save the buffalo rarely kept up the pace.[36]

Canadian authorities began to call upon the last of the free Lakota to return to the United States. The government denied Sitting Bull's requests for aid on behalf of the hungry and sick. He watched the bison herds dwindle and the refugee camps slowly disintegrate. His distrust of the Long Knives—and, perhaps, his need to reach consensus among his people before committing to any particular plan of action—delayed a final return to the other side of the "holy line." Nightmares of prison bars, iron chains, and hanging gallows disturbed him for months as he prepared to lay down his life eventually. However bleak his future, he decided to risk possible execution so that the destitute might live on the Great Sioux Reservation. He joined with over forty families and journeyed southward to Fort Buford in the Montana Territory. On July 20, 1881, he directed his son Crow Foot to hand a loaded Winchester to the US Army officer in command. After making the gesture, he spoke: "I wish to be remembered as the last man of my tribe to surrender my rifle." Suffering an eye infection, he wore a pair of goggles while undertaking a short trip aboard a downriver steamer named the *General Sherman*. As a symbol of peacefulness, he carried a three-and-a-half-foot long pipe. On a brief stop, he toured the territorial town of Bismarck before continuing the boat ride to Fort Yates. The assassination of US President James A. Garfield and the murder of Sicangu Chief Spotted Tail came to his attention. He dreaded his own fate. Word-of-mouth promises of amnesty and pardons were not reliable, for his military record in the Great Sioux War earned him the abiding enmity of officials in Washington DC. Dispatched to Fort Randall in the Dakota Territory, he remained a prisoner of war for nearly two years.[37]

Sitting Bull's time as a prisoner of war revealed his capacity for adaptation. With the thirty-two lodges of his band under the eye of armed sentinels, he found ways to tolerate the constraints around the military outpost. He accepted the constant surveillance of the bluecoats as well as the rations of pork, hardtack, and flour they provided. From nearby agencies, former headmen sought his advice. The inquisitive press reported on his routines, which involved occasional interviews and photographs. He began writing his Anglicized name in cursive script and signed autographs for tourists. He met with several visitors to the prison camp, including Reverend John P. Williamson, a Presbyterian missionary serving at the nearby Yankton agency; Thomas H. Tibbles, an Indian rights activist at the Rosebud agency; Alice Fletcher, an ethnologist investigating the customs of Indigenous societies; and scores of curiosity seekers. He expressed particular affinity for Rudolf Cronau, a visiting German writer and artist, who staged an exhibition of Native American portraits at Fort Randall. He befriended almost anyone willing to treat him with respect and kindness, which signified a kind of diplomatic posture that enabled him to hone his messages for a wider audience.[38]

After reviewing a decade-old collection of "ledger art" depicting his war deeds, Sitting Bull created at least three autobiographical sets of drawings at Fort Randall. He used paper, pencil, ink, and watercolors, likely obtained from the post trader, Daniel L. Pratt, for the first set of drawings. Acting

Introduction: A Lakota Life

Sitting Bull, half-length portrait, seated, facing front, holding calumet, 1881.

on behalf of Brigadier General John C. Smith, Lieutenant Wallace Tear of the Twenty-Fifth Infantry traded some blankets and clothing to Sitting Bull for yet another set of drawings; Sitting Bull gave the blankets and clothes to Lakota children. Sitting Bull presented his third set of drawings to the youngest daughter of the regimental quartermaster, Captain Horace Quimby, whose wife, Martha, often brought food to the prison camp. Aided by interpreters and scribes at the military outpost, Sitting Bull told his own story with flair.[39]

With Sitting Bull detained at Fort Randall, the US government expanded the "white man's road" across the northern Great Plains. Inside the Department of the Interior, the Office of Indian Affairs issued edicts intended to force the cultural assimilation of all Native Americans. Though the *hochoka* continued to represent the center of gravity for the Lakota way of life, federal agents wielded greater control over tribal leadership. As traditional lines of authority crumbled, the *itancan* at the various Lakota agencies were belittled as "relics of barbarism." Police units, whose badges spawned the nickname *ceska maza*, or "metal breasts," assumed responsibility for law enforcement at each agency. Missionaries, churches, and schools proliferated along the tributaries of the upper Missouri, generating mixed results. Though undermined by the organization of the reservation system, aspects of "Indianness" contributed to a distinct sense of collective identity. Over the years, Sitting Bull advised his people: "When you find anything good in the white man's road, pick it up; but when you find something bad, or that turns out bad, drop it, leave it alone."[40]

Standing Rock

Assigned to the Standing Rock agency in 1883, Sitting Bull lived peacefully in a log cabin along the Grand River. A brother-in-law, Gray Eagle, offered him shelter within the small settlement some forty miles southwest of Fort Yates. Sitting Bull's general health declined while he was there, and he complained about constant fatigue. His face appeared drawn on one side; one of his eyes twitched. He did not expect to live for long. Designated a district farmer, he passed the days tending horses, cattle, and chickens while cultivating oats, corn, and potatoes. Family members worked the fields too.

He continued to raise five children in his household, including two pairs of twins—all boys—as well as a girl named Standing Holy. His wives gave birth to two more children. Unfortunately, his nineteen-year-old daughter, Walks Looking, died from a disease. A number of grandchildren kept him thinking about the future. Although distrustful of the US government, he urged the boys and girls to attend a nearby Christian day school in order to learn how to read and to write. He gave no indication of a decline in Lakota spiritualism. With the sun dance and "pagan practices" prohibited at Standing Rock, he looked for complementary expressions of power and knowledge in the established churches. For example, he donned a crucifix on occasion. Perhaps he appreciated the Virgin Mary as a human incarnation of Divine Motherhood to the extent that she was syncretic with a sacred Lakota entity known as White Buffalo Calf Maiden. The dogmas of religiosity, however, perplexed him. He surmised wryly: "The Sioux were better Christians before they ever heard of Christ than the white men are now."[41]

Meanwhile, Sitting Bull came to terms with a world turned upside down. James "White Hair" McLaughlin, the Standing Rock agent, dismissed him as "an Indian of very mediocre ability" and bemoaned "his sheer obstinacy and stubborn tenacity." Complying with an agency demand for law and order, Sitting Bull quietly directed One Bull, his nephew, to join the police force. His sympathizers at Standing Rock remained deferential, even though chieftains such as Four Horns and Black Moon descended into idleness; both were dead by the end of the decade. Gall, now a corpulent "boss" farmer, gained wider influence among the Hunkpapa. Considered a "good talker," a Sihasapa named Charging Bear, or John Grass, relished the agent's patronage. As at other agencies, Standing Rock formed an Indian court as a weapon against "demoralizing and barbarous" customs. Whatever the discretion of the judges, the list of Indian "offenses" included polygamy, healing ceremonies, and traditional feasts. Sitting Bull continued to assemble the Silent Eaters, who vowed in secret meetings to protect him at all costs.[42]

Sitting Bull became a minor celebrity during the Gilded Age. Agent McLaughlin permitted him to participate in a grand parade celebrating the recognition of Bismarck as the capital of the Dakota Territory. Then, in 1884, the legendary Lakota appeared in a traveling exhibition run by

Minnesota businessman Alvaren Allen. His presence stirred the passions of audiences. He sang, danced, and spoke at a venue in Philadelphia, Pennsylvania; there, Luther Standing Bear, an Oglala youth enrolled at the Carlisle Indian Industrial School, met him following the performance. The next year Sitting Bull was allowed to join Buffalo Bill's Wild West, a traveling vaudevillian show organized by William F. Cody. Possibly intrigued by the staging of the Plains Indian wars, he participated in a four-month tour, earning $50 a week and a bonus of $125 for appearing on a light gray horse in the arena. He stood next to "Long Hair" Cody for a publicity picture, which featured the two in an affable pose. He favored "Little Sure Shot," the performer Annie Oakley, and unofficially adopted her as a daughter. While hearing boos and hisses from rowdy crowds, he profited from the sale of autographs and photocards in more than a dozen cities. He brought a portion of his earnings home as income but gave away the rest to the "street urchins" he encountered. He stayed with the troupe until the end of the season, eager to visit with the Great Father in Washington DC. Cody made a fortune from the extravaganzas, but Agent McLaughlin abruptly halted Sitting Bull's career in show business.[43]

Upon returning to Standing Rock, Sitting Bull tried to assert his authority over all the agency's figureheads. He called for a revival of the sun dances and other suppressed conventions. He joined a Sioux delegation on a journey to the Crow Reservation, where the traditional enemies shook hands, talked about politics, and enjoyed festivities near the Little Bighorn River. In 1887, Sitting Bull learned that the Dawes Act legalized a zealous scheme for the allotment of reservation lands in severalty to tribal members. He chafed at the partitioning of the Lakota lands into six reservations: Standing Rock, Pine Ridge, Rosebud, Cheyenne River, Crow Creek, and Lower Brule. He denounced the injustices of the Sioux Agreement, which ruthlessly diminished tribal landholding and opened an additional nine million acres for non-Indian settlement. As each cut reduced independence and sustainability for the Plains Indians, his malaise deepened. Sitting Bull joined another Sioux delegation on a train trip to the national capital. There, he entered the White House to shake hands with US President Grover Cleveland but failed to gain support for the delegation's counterproposals. On November 2, 1889, North and South Dakota became new states, entering the Union together. His sense of fatalism growing, Sitting Bull received a dire warning

Sitting Bull and Buffalo Bill.

from a meadowlark that he would die at the hands of the Lakota. "I would rather die an Indian," he prophetically remarked to friends at Standing Rock, "than live a white man."[44]

Sitting Bull perceived another menacing omen: alcohol abuse. He said that intoxication appeared to "crumple up" or deaden the soul and that his people should "separate themselves from drunkards." He refused to even taste whiskey and disdained its influence over others. Perhaps the sacramental use of wine for a Catholic communion was acceptable, but he posited that the frequent consumption of distilled spirits by the Long Knives may have helped his warriors defeat them at the Little Bighorn River. Whiskey seemed to replace the buffalo as a priority during the Gilded Age, giving "no hope for the Indians." In fact, observed Sitting Bull, prairie winds and rain showers would need to purify the souls of human beings for hundreds of years in order to prevent the odor of alcohol from making the afterlife so noxious.[45]

In 1889, the plight of the Sioux garnered the attention of the National Indian Defense Association, or NIDA, a philanthropic clique in Washington DC derided by the press for its "sentimentalists." One member, a pious, wealthy New Yorker who called herself Catherine Weldon, visited Standing Rock that summer. Previously known as Caroline Schlatter, she was a divorcée with an eleven-year-old son, Christie. The Hunkpapa dubbed her "Woman Walking Ahead." Newspapermen scorned her as "Sitting Bull's Squaw." After hearing about her "high words" against the machinations of Agent McLaughlin, Sitting Bull invited her and her son to stay at his cabin for a time. While sharing domestic responsibilities with his wives, she purchased provisions, penned correspondence, and counseled him. She urged Sitting Bull and other recruits to become members of the NIDA. One of her oil paintings—a portrait of the aging chief—hung on his cabin wall. Whatever the nature of her relationship with him, she lamented that so many Indians "reject the true Christ about whom I spoke." Her crusade came to an end in late 1890, when she sadly packed her belongings to leave the Dakotas. Sitting Bull escorted her and her son to Fort Yates, saying farewell to them for the last time.[46]

Sitting Bull foresaw grave dangers at Standing Rock, as the apocalyptic mood seemed palpable. The *wasi'chus* insisted on a doctrine of settler sovereignty, which gave them property and rights in newly organized states while simultaneously dispossessing and impoverishing the Indigenous populations. Reservation communities fractured into "progressive" and "nonprogressive" elements, shattering cultural cohesiveness. Whooping cough, measles, influenza, and other maladies took a heavy toll on life, especially among families with malnourished children or ailing elders. Due to restricted mobility, the limited access to water supplies caused alarm. Soaring temperatures accompanied a midsummer drought that devastated the farmlands and livestock. Crop failures and ration reductions exacerbated food shortages. The bison herds no longer thundered across the North American grasslands. In the absence of federal or state relief measures, fears of famine intensified. The corralled hunters and gatherers struggled to make sense of the evil that had befallen them and pondered the ominous signs of a last sunset. Then, in the far western sections of the United States, a Paiute holy man named Wovoka shared a prophecy: a new millennium was coming.[47]

Likely influenced by Christian teachings, Wovoka dreamt of the Messiah during a solar eclipse. The heterodox messages of "God's red son" echoed the Biblical texts referenced by clergy and missionaries. Returning from pilgrimages to meet the prophet, a cadre of Lakota believers mentioned seeing Jesus or the Christ in their communal reporting. Some indicated that Wovoka himself was a savior, while others spoke of a heavenly paragon. Millenarianism promoted a belief in the imminent collapse of a corrupt, fallen world followed by its replacement with a just, utopian order. Even if particular elements of "God's kingdom" may have resonated with the First Peoples of North America, the intolerance evinced by religious authorities made the coexistence of belief systems difficult. According to church officials, 4,757 souls among 18,000 or so Lakota had converted to Christianity by 1889. In spite of the rampant hunger and thirst, federal agents would withhold government-issued supplies from individuals refusing to attend church. The woebegone populace stood at a crossroads. By relaying a code for living, Wovoka's Ghost Dance movement pointed a generation in crisis toward both a traditional path and a pan-Indian future.[48]

On October 9, 1890, Kicking Bear, a Miniconjou Sioux from the Cheyenne River Reservation and trusted relative of Sitting Bull, came to Standing Rock with the "good news" from Wovoka: participation in the *wanagi wachipi ki*, or "spirit dance" ceremony, induced a visionary experience. Through this ceremony the "chosen people" of *Wakantanka* could envisage the return of the buffalo, deer, and elk as well as the resurrection of deceased kith and kin. The great transformation revealed in these visions would revive the prairies with a rich layer of sod; the rivers would swell with fresh water; the skies would brighten with new hope. A new Heaven and new Earth would restore peace and justice to the "red children," who would no longer fear the aggression of the "white man." A blessed "ghost shirt" would protect them from deadly weaponry, or so Kicking Bear claimed.[49] At first skeptical of this magical thinking, Sitting Bull planted a prayer tree north of his cabin and became the "chief apostle" of the dances at the Grand River camp. As docile students abandoned the reservation schools and awaited the final countdown, he appointed a dance director for the small settlement. He painted his face and carried his medicine bag, wearing what appeared to be a "ghost shirt" decorated with a red cross. The zealous crowds near his cabin began to increase in number, as many yearned to experience the forbidden sun dances once again. Sitting Bull's interest in these messianic notions invigorated a last-ditch effort to renew Lakota ways.[50]

From dawn to dusk, Sitting Bull watched over the multitude, fasted, and prayed for guidance. He allegedly broke his sacred peace pipe in the presence of the assembled Ghost Dancers, but rumors of his return to militancy may have been false. He refused to go to the agency headquarters to accept the paltry rations and, in the spirit of the *wanagi wachipi ki*, urged the Lakota men, women, and children to link hand to hand in a vibrant ring of motion—jumping, whirling, and singing—until they collapsed in the circle of brush arbors. While visiting the Grand River camp, Agent McLaughlin observed that Sitting Bull's body appeared diminished from deprivation and exertion, reduced to mere skin and bones. He walked from his cabin to the tents wearing little more than a breechclout and moccasins, wrapping himself in a blanket in preparation for a "feast with the ghosts." His wits remained as sharp as ever, however, and he conducted nightly séances and ministered to an ecstatic throng gathered at the river. His herald, Bull Ghost, announced a series of enchanting messages that arrived telepathically. Sitting Bull insisted that participants in the *wanagi wachipi ki* cleanse themselves every morning with a vapor bath in small sweat lodges. The participants remained in the heat as long as their bodies could endure it, only emerging from an *inikagapi* when ready to be anointed by the "high priest." Sitting Bull's followers grew to as many as two hundred in number.[51]

Mary C. Collins, a Congregationalist missionary at Standing Rock, complained that Sitting Bull was leading her converts back into "heathendom." Regardless of their cultural differences, he called her *Wenonah*, or "first daughter," out of respect and honored her as a "medicine woman." She referred to him as the "head chief," acknowledging that he possessed a "very indefinable power" among the Lakota. After a singing of "Nearer My God to Thee," her sermonizing continued inside his "holy tent." She marveled at his comprehension of the Bible but scolded him for preaching that "the Christ had come for the Indians now and that they alone would rise." When dry weather threatened their harvests, she watched as he took a buffalo skin, waved it through the air, placed it upon the ground, and performed gestures with his hands. To her astonishment, it rained. As winter approached that year, she recalled that he claimed the miraculous ability to feed his followers no matter the season. "Yes, my people," he predicted before a surging congregation at the Grand River camp, "you can dance all the winter this year, the sun will shine warmly, and the weather will be fair."[52]

The Standing Rock police attempted to intimidate Sitting Bull, who responded calmly by saying the gatherings would wane in time. Lawman One Bull learned that most of Sitting Bull's followers expected a climactic regeneration to occur during the spring months; he also heard that Indians who doubted the prophecy might turn into dogs. One Bull lost his job with the police force following his own participation in the Ghost Dance circles. One Bull's pregnant wife Red Whirlwind and his daughter Rosie continued to reside at his uncle's cabin. With rations scarce or inedible, One Bull earned a few dollars by hauling freight from a railroad town to the agency warehouse. He frequented the trader's store. He kept an eye on his uncle at the riverside while hearing about the coming of bluecoats from the Heart River, Slim Buttes, and Fort Sully. Even if doubts arose about his fidelity, he outfitted a horse for carrying loads on short hauls and attempted to get back home on wintery nights. Though lacking definitive proof, a few voices opined that One Bull betrayed Sitting Bull by spying on behalf of federal agents.[53]

Because Sitting Bull stood among the "leaders of disaffection," Agent McLaughlin worried that the Lakota might attempt to orchestrate a major breakout from Standing Rock. Around this time young and old Indians left the Pine Ridge, Rosebud, and Cheyenne River Reservations to gather anxiously at a tableland refuge identified as "the Stronghold." Short Bull, an ally of Kicking Bear and a disciple of Wovoka's "gospel," invited the *wichásha wakán* to the site. But Sitting Bull remained with his inner circle at the Grand River camp and posed no danger to anyone. In late 1890, US

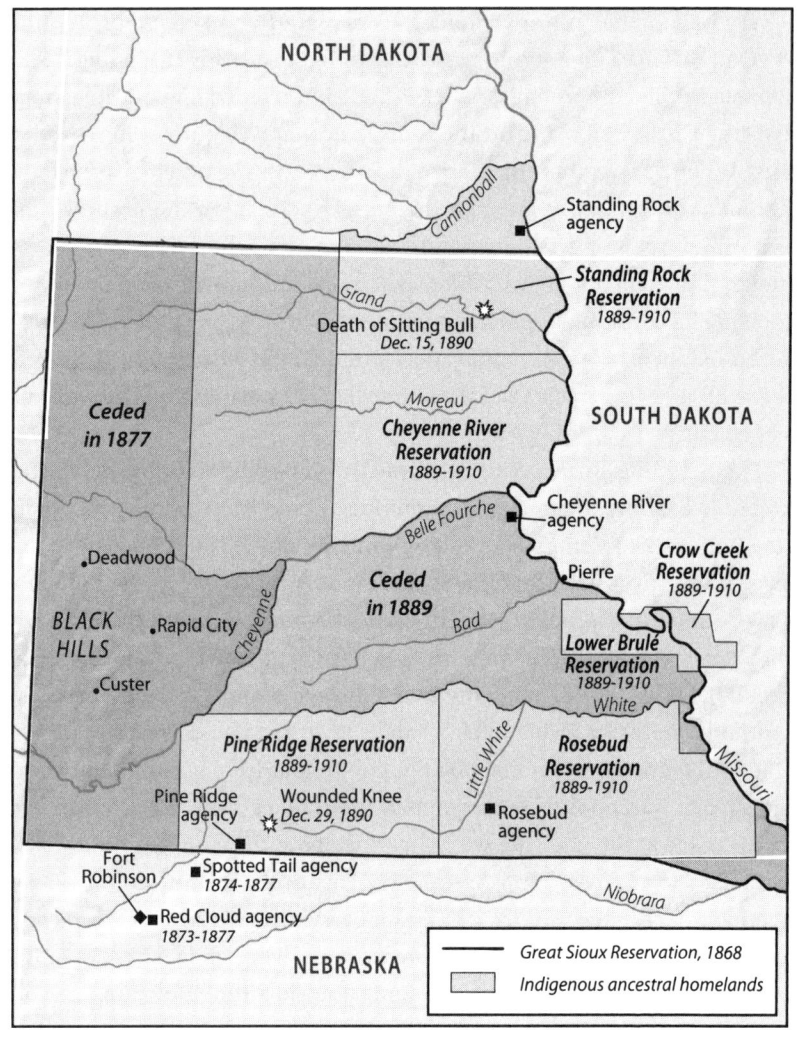

Map of Lakota Reservations, 1890.

President Benjamin Harrison dispatched approximately seven thousand soldiers to assist the agencies in thwarting a perceived insurrection. Secretary of the Interior John W. Noble granted immediate jurisdiction to the US Army for the emergency crackdown. Major General Miles, now commanding the Military Division of the Missouri, authorized "Buffalo Bill" Cody to "secure the person of Sitting Bull," but his order was rescinded. Within days, Colonel William F. Drum at Fort Yates received a similar order. Working in concert with the armed forces—and without providing legitimate substantiation for formal charges—Agent McLaughlin directed loyal members of the Standing Rock police to arrest Sitting Bull. "You must not let him escape under any circumstances," stated the postscript of his letter to the police officers. Evidently, Sitting Bull intended to visit "the Stronghold" that winter and had notified Agent McLaughlin of his pending departure.[54]

The air turned cold on Monday, December 15, 1890. The sky was dark and hazy at daybreak. A mix of sleet and rain fell on the ground. Equipped with a Hotchkiss gun and a Gatling gun from Fort Yates, Captain Edmond G. Fechet of the Eighth Cavalry positioned troops near the Oak Creek crossing of the road approaching the Grand River camp. At least forty-three mounted members of a Lakota police unit rode to Sitting Bull's cabin. Three officers burst through the entry, grabbed the slumbering chief from his bed, and pushed him toward the door. Stumbling forward in moccasins, he sang a farewell song to his family. Aroused by the sound of barking dogs, over a hundred dancers from the camp rallied to defend him. "Then I will not go," he said at the doorway—likely his last words. One of his wives, Four Robes, noticed that the well-armed lawmen "smelled of whiskey," as one of his confidantes, Catch the Bear, bolted toward them. Closing their ranks, the police shot Sitting Bull seven times. Lieutenant Bull Head shot him in the chest, while Sergeant Red Tomahawk shot him in the head. Restrained and unarmed, he fell in front of his cabin. His teenage son Crow Foot was also killed in cold blood by the gunfire. The scrum turned into chaos, and the frightened bystanders fled for their lives in all directions. The dying and wounded writhed on the ground. Within a fifty-yard radius of the cabin, Sitting Bull, seven of his entourage, and four officers died immediately. At least two more officers were mortally wounded. Sadly, Sitting Bull's final vision of his own death had come to pass.[55]

A Lakota winter count later documented the crime scene, revealing hoofprints and bullet casings around Sitting Bull's cabin.[56] With the lifting of the morning fog came speculation, accusations, and curses. Within an hour or so of the shooting a blue skirmish line moved into position to secure the perimeter, but damage to the premises suggests that plundering and pillaging ensued. US soldiers heard wailing all around as the deceased Lakota's blood pooled at their feet. The lifeless victim sprawled before them. Holy Medicine, a slain policeman's brother, smashed Sitting Bull's face with a blow from a wooden neck yoke. A member of the military outfit interceded to halt further mutilation. Enlisted men loaded the corpses into an old farm wagon for transport to Fort Yates. During a postmortem inspection of Sitting Bull's body, an attending physician took a piece of his hair and stole his leggings. Sitting Bull's remains were wrapped in a blanket and placed inside a pine box, which was then buried in the northwest corner of the post cemetery. No funeral or ceremony consecrated the spot. To mark the solitary gravesite, a plain headboard of wood was painted with stenciled black words: "Sitting Bull, Indian." Officially, the military records confirmed the interment on December 17, 1890.[57]

The killing of Sitting Bull set the stage for more bloodshed in the coming days. Several of his dismayed associates raced to the camp of Spotted Elk, who was known also as Big Foot. Responding to telegrams, General Miles issued a series of orders from his Chicago headquarters to stop the "outbreak" in the northern Great Plains. There were some four thousand Ghost Dancers among the Lakota—that is, as much as one-quarter of the whole population but in no sense a majority. Of course, the regulars, auxiliaries, and policemen outnumbered possible insurgents in a confrontation. On December 29, 1890, the Seventh Cavalry detained Big Foot and his 340 campers at Wounded Knee Creek. The Lakota hoisted a white flag beneath a battery of four Hotchkiss guns situated on a hilltop. Then, when a shot rang out, the cordon of 470 US soldiers opened fire with rifles, revolvers, and artillery. What had started as a possible—though mostly one-sided— battle instantly became a massacre. For example, point-blank executions and shocking atrocities occurred in a gulch. At least 270 Lakota perished across the killing field, likely half of which were women and children. In the aftermath, a winter storm covered the ground with a blanket of snow. On New Year's Day of 1891, military details began to collect the frozen, mangled bodies of the dead.[58]

Sitting Bull's people could do little to hold back the settler sovereignty that had defined the concerted efforts of the US government to diminish the *Očhéthi Šakówiŋ*. With each wave of colonization, the *wasi'chus* insisted on the right to conquer native space one way or another. Even though "ethnic cleansing" was not a term in use before the twentieth century, its definition certainly applies to the widespread, systematic assault directed by governmental functionaries against a stateless group with durable claims to an ancestral homeland. The bison ecology had sustained the Lakota way of life for ages, but the demise of self-sufficiency made them largely dependent on an inept bureaucracy for sustenance. Isolation and starvation became their lot. An array of coercive measures forced them to give up communal landholdings and to survive on splintered reservations in the northern Great Plains. Officials in Washington DC left behind a trail of broken treaties that resulted in frontier violence from the Black Hills to Wounded Knee. Enflaming passions again and again, policymakers dismissed a "vanishing race." Even if reforms promised better days, the 1924 grant of citizenship to all Native Americans in the country came far too late to prevent the injustices. In a long-delayed judicial opinion, the US Supreme Court mentioned "Sitting Bull's notable victory" at the Little Bighorn while upholding an award of more than $100 million to the Siouxan litigants. Because some Siouxan voices wanted not money but the return of the taken territory, the funds were never paid out, instead accruing interest in a Bureau of Indian Affairs account.[59]

The US government proclaimed an end to the "Last Indian War," yet the bones of Sitting Bull did not lie undisturbed. On April 7, 1953, Clarence Gray Eagle, the son of Sitting Bull's brother-in-law, led a disinterment party to the Fort Yates gravesite. They exhumed what they could find, which they then reburied in a heavy concrete vault near Mobridge, South Dakota. A large memorial bust at the burial site overlooks the Missouri River, despite doubts about the actual final resting place of Sitting Bull. Some accounts note that his skull, shoulder blade, ribs, and other pieces had been removed earlier from the Fort Yates gravesite. Others insist that skeletal fragments lie in multiple spots. The whole truth may never be known.[60]

Sitting Bull's name is among the best known of any Native American leader; his story circulated around the world. His demonstration of spiritual strength illustrated the Lakota virtues of bravery, fortitude, generosity, and wisdom. While mobilizing Indigenous communities during the twilight of the Plains Indian wars, he faced long odds in an epic struggle for living space. His resiliency emboldened a resistance movement against the military posture of the United States, which all too often pushed aside tribal groups across the North American continent. Holding on to a deeply rooted existence, he focused on a holy mission to save—in the words of

34 Introduction: A Lakota Life

"Let us put our minds together and see what life we will make for our children."

the Siouxan speakers—*mitakuye oyasin*, or "all my relatives." His battles against Manifest Destiny made him a heroic symbol of an unbroken past, albeit with an exalted "chieftainship." He perceived what others could not see because of his farsightedness regarding the changes in the land. Even though his death came with a sudden burst of gunfire, his visions of self-determination gave future generations the chance to imagine a road ahead. The Standing Rock Sioux Tribal Council chartered Sitting Bull College, where one of his warbonnets is kept on display. "Let us put our minds together," he appears to say on a graphic poster of the late twentieth century, "and see what life we will make for our children."[61] In that heartfelt sense, Sitting Bull's kind of war never ends.

NOTE ON SOURCES AND METHODS

The histories of the Plains Indian wars document the First Peoples of North America, occasionally attributing quotes to Sitting Bull, a Lakota Sioux leader. Scholars have identified the recorded sayings of a nonliterate person, who achieved remarkable prominence in defense of an ancestral homeland. Nevertheless, the exact wording remains difficult to untangle from distortions and errata that obscure what is knowable. The search for authentic Native American perspectives has unearthed pieces that bear the imprint of orality: short, provocative, memorable, oft-repeated phrases, anecdotes, songs, and prayers. Interdisciplinary studies have demonstrated how an oral tradition endeavors to retain the essence or gist of utterances. Vetting assigns levels of reliability and validity to the available evidence, especially if corroboration exists in surviving accounts. Since archives, libraries, and museums evaluate scores of literary artifacts, careful discernment gives credence to discourses that otherwise may be apocryphal.

The coherence of Sitting Bull's discourse survives in the partial and fragmentary evidence of a remembered past. Unfortunately, the unsystematic elaboration of observations that one only hopes to be accurate contributes to the acceptance of misinformation. Even the finest transmitters of an oral tradition do not ordinarily recall a long word-for-word recitation with precision. It can be likened to an experiment with whispers in a proverbial "telephone game." The absence or scarcity of written records can undermine confidence in storytelling, but the impressions of a speaker remain noteworthy. Whenever initial statements appear verifiable, key voices gain a sympathetic audience through the cultural production, dissemination, and circulation of historical memories. Academic inquiries into verbiage, innuendo, gestures, play, code-switching, and silences help to clarify the intentions and meanings of a transcribed text.

An effective strategy for the presentation of any text is to appreciate its wider context. For example, a host of writers have explored the Battle of the Little Bighorn from the different sides of "Custer's Hill." Drawn to a place also known as the Greasy Grass, some have unearthed significant clues for the substantiation of overlooked claims. Almost any disclosure that surprises or embarrasses authorities is liable to earn attention, although unpalatable details seldom make it into an official record. One can survey the governmental reports to see if a possible source betrays a pattern of inconsistencies about geography, forces, or circumstances. Furthermore, the journalistic coverage by newspaper correspondents on assignment deserves close scrutiny. Hearsay recounted years after an event should be doubted, yet a verbatim transcription can be compelling if cross-referenced and confirmed by a series of interrogations. The transparency of citations and bibliographies enhance the practices of textual analysis, which inform a historian's approach to puzzling attributions.

Many different people influenced the attributions of an Indigene. Tribal leaders sent word outside their inner circles, occasionally authorizing couriers to "telegraph" messages to others. Whereas the rare communication passed through several mouths, ears, and minds, it was memorialized on loose sheets of paper at campgrounds, military outposts, or agency offices. Firsthand renderings also appeared in the compilations of Plains Indian "ledger art," which traveled hundreds of miles before arriving at a final destination. Producing a "first draft of history," a New York journalist named Willis Fletcher Johnson assembled *The Red Record of the Sioux: Life of Sitting Bull and History of the Indian War of 1890–91* (1891). In the wake of the Gilded Age, histories too often relegated the material to the realm of fanciful legends.

Composing under the pseudonym of Stanley Vestal, Walter S. Campbell filled a gap in the histories of the North American frontier and borderlands. He taught literature and creative writing at the University of Oklahoma, where the Western History Collections catalogued his research notes, professional correspondence, and assorted manuscripts. Beginning in the 1920s, he made visits to the Standing Rock Reservation in South Dakota. While enlisting Sitting Bull's relatives for field research, he paid money to retain translators and to organize consultations. Notably, Henry Oscar One Bull, the second son of Sitting Bull's sister Good Feather Woman and Makes Room, a Miniconjou chieftain, had been born in 1853. His older brother, Joseph White Bull, had been born in 1849. Both siblings collaborated with Campbell until they died in 1947. Even if uncertain about cultural and linguistic subtleties, he recognized the contributions of thirty-four Lakota informants. Their joint efforts inspired his original biography, *Sitting Bull: Champion of the Sioux* (1932). The revised editions lacked ample footnoting, yet the "new" sources established the foundation of Campbell's work.

More than fifty years later, historian Robert Utley crafted a masterpiece, *The Lance and the Shield: The Life and Times of Sitting Bull* (1993), which exploited Campbell's collection. His award-winning book also cited a trove of documents in the US National Archives as well as reports by Canadian government officials. While acknowledging social and intellectual differences, he stressed the logic of Sitting Bull's actions during the Great Sioux War.

A mix of writers continue to refine the historical canons of a new millennium. To name just one, a great-grandson of Sitting Bull, Ernie LaPointe, shared personal insights about his great-grandfather in *Sitting Bull: His Life and Legacy* (2011). Based on recollections from family lore, it was written by a lineal descendant born on the Pine Ridge Reservation.

Focused upon these and other writings, I have undertaken a quest to locate and to preserve the sentiments of Sitting Bull for a "red-letter" anthology. Whenever considering the credibility of any source, the first question for a historian is about its content: What is the source saying? Moreover, historical research and methods deem a second question worth asking: What is the source doing when presented to an audience? Within the broad sweep of history, my aim is to comprehend an extraordinary human being through his own words. A combination of first-person testimony began with a Lakota Sioux, who spoke for those struggling against conquest. The excerpts of primary and secondary sources reveal a quotable Sitting Bull in a time for war.

Sorting through the most likely quotations, I am guided by three rules of evidence. First, only elocutions traceable to a time and place of transmission can have originated with Sitting Bull. Second, proximate interlocutors of an articulation would have retained the substance of what had been spoken if they were assisted by a translator or were familiar with his native tongue. Third, a close or similar transcription of a sample must have merited two or more attestations in order to give sufficient assurance about the plausibility of an embedding. With these three rules uppermost in mind, I am sharing with readers what Sitting Bull said.

With regard to editing what has been said, my policy is to show the work. Thucydides, the model of an ancient Greek historian, famously handled the dialogue of various speakers by making them say whatever seemed appropriate to him. Sitting Bull, however, seized opportunities to speak for himself. In spite of confusion and discrepancies in sourcing, historians try to get as close as possible to the general scope of the exact wording. Interventions involve only minor alterations to typography, formatting, paragraphing, spelling, capitalization, and punctuation, which address momentary lapses, awkward syntax, or sleights of hand. The presence of inconsistent or quaint grammar warrants caution, just as an unclear or omitted comment calls for a brief insertion with brackets. Relevant asides appear in parenthesis. If a passage is digressive, interrupted, or truncated, then the occasional ellipses indicates a subjective breakage within a sentence or a paragraph. For any given entry, I avoid excessive markings so that the word flow of an extract stays even and accessible. The overall objective in this kind of editorial process is to facilitate a curated reading of a concise history with documents.

The documents from a bygone era utilize terminology that can be problematic. The term "Indians" was a conception of Europeans, while recent writers choose to employ "Native Americans," "First Peoples," or "Indigenous." The term "Sioux" encompasses myriad bands and tribal groups, including the "Teton" or "Lakota." While a mixture of nomenclature has been associated with residual populations, no interpretation of languages is free from social construction. My preference is to use appropriate parlance for each document.

My formulation of the documents respects a Lakota tradition: the sacred number four. There are four annual seasons, four lunar phases, four cardinal directions, and four basic elements. Thus, the documents of the Lakota Sioux leader resonate with four chronological themes: Emergence, Battleground, Border Crossings, and Standing Rock.

PART 1

EMERGENCE

> White Buffalo Calf Maiden embodies a sacred entity revered by many generations of the Lakota Sioux. Siouxan visionary traditions venerate a plethora of extraordinary beings such as Grandfather Buffalo, Elk, Bear, Rock, Wind, Moon, and Sun, but she is the only anthropomorphic figure of the pantheon. She appeared to Sitting Bull's ancestors ages ago to teach them how to maintain the "good ways" of Wakantanka. It was said that she disappeared into a misty haze upon a hilltop, where her transformation into a white buffalo calf occurred on the other side. Several variations of the Sacred Woman or White She-Buffalo theme emerged with the ancient myths of the Plains Indians. Whereas one of her ceremonial symbols is the sacred pipe, she also became known as a goddess of tobacco. As long as the tribal councils continued to perform the seven ceremonies that she taught, they acknowledged the rituals that constituted the "Buffalo Nation." Undoubtedly, the family of Sitting Bull repeated her story around campfires before and after his birth. The teachings were preserved in a condensed form by Frances Densmore, an American ethnomusicologist, who collected "Teton" songs and memorabilia for an official publication in 1918. The primary Lakota informant for a common version was John Lone Man, and Robert P. Higheagle provided the recorded English translation.[1]

A council was called, and two young men were selected to go in quest of buffalo and other game. They started on foot. When they were out of sight, they each went in a different direction but met again at a place which they had agreed upon. While they were planning what to do, there appeared from the west a solitary object advancing toward them. It did not look like a buffalo; it looked more like a human being than anything else. They could not make out what it was, but it was coming rapidly. Both considered themselves brave, so they concluded that they would face whatever it might be. They stood still and gazed at it very eagerly. At last they saw that it was a beautiful young maiden. She wore a beautiful fringed buckskin dress, leggings, and moccasins. Her hair was hanging loose except at the left side, where was tied a tuft of shedded buffalo hair. In her right hand, she carried a fan made of flat sage. Her face was painted with red vertical stripes. Not knowing what to do or say, they said nothing to her.

She spoke first thus:

"I am sent by the Buffalo tribe to visit the people you represent. You have been chosen to perform a difficult task. It is right that you should try to carry out the wishes of your people, and you must try to accomplish your purpose. Go home and tell the chief and headmen to put up a special lodge in the middle of the camp circle, with the door of the lodge and the entrance into the camp toward the direction where the sun rolls off the Earth. Let them spread sage at the place of honor, and back of the fireplace let a small square place be prepared. Back of this and the sage let a certain frame, or rack, be made. Right in front of the rack a buffalo skull should be placed. I have something of importance to present to the tribe, which will have a great deal to do with their future welfare. I shall be in the camp about sunrise."

While she was thus speaking to the young men, one of them had impure thoughts. A cloud came down and enveloped this young man. When the cloud left the Earth, the young man was left there—only a skeleton. The Maiden commanded the other young man to turn his back toward her and face in the direction of the camp, then to start for home. He was ordered not to look back.

When the young man came in sight of the camp, he ran in a zigzag course, this being a signal required of such parties on returning home from a searching or scouting expedition. The people in the camp were on the alert for the signal, and preparations were begun at once to escort the party home. Just outside the council lodge, in front of the door, an old man qualified to perform the ceremony was waiting anxiously for the party. He knelt in the direction of the coming of the party to receive the report of the expedition. A row of old men were kneeling behind him. The young man arrived at the lodge. Great curiosity was shown by the people on account of the missing member of the party. The report was made, and the people received it with enthusiasm.

The special lodge was made, and the other requirements were carried out. The crier announced in the whole camp what was to take place on the following morning. Great preparations were made for the occasion. Early the next morning, at daybreak, men, women, and children assembled around the special lodge. Young men who were known to bear unblemished characters were chosen to escort the Maiden into the camp. Promptly at sunrise she was in sight. Everybody was anxious. All eyes were fixed on the Maiden. Slowly she walked into the camp. She was dressed as when she first appeared to the two young men except that instead of the sage fan she carried a pipe—the stem was carried with her right hand and the bowl with the left.

The chief, who was qualified and authorized to receive the guest on behalf of the Sioux tribe, sat outside, right in front of the door of the lodge, facing the direction of the coming of the Maiden. When she was at the door, the chief stepped aside and made room for her to enter. She entered the lodge, went to the left of the door, and was seated at the place of honor.

The chief made a speech welcoming the Maiden as follows:

"My dear relatives: This day *Wakantanka* has again looked down and smiled upon us by sending us this young Maiden, whom we shall recognize and consider a sister. She has come to our rescue, just as we are in great need. *Wakantanka* wishes us to live. This day we lift up our eyes to the sun, the giver of light, that opens our eyes and gives us this beautiful day to see our visiting sister. Sister, we are glad that you have come to us and trust that whatever message you have brought we may be able to abide by it. We are poor, but we have a great respect to [give to] visitors, especially relatives. It is our custom to serve our guests with some special food. We are at present needy, and all we have to offer you is water that falls from the clouds. Take it, drink it, and remember that we are very poor."

Then braided sweet grass was dipped into a buffalo horn containing rain water and was offered to the Maiden. The chief said: "Sister, we are now ready to hear the good message you have brought." The pipe, which was in the hands of the Maiden, was lowered and placed on the rack. Then the Maiden sipped the water from the sweet grass.

Then taking up the pipe again, she arose and said:

"My relatives, brothers and sisters: *Wakantanka* has looked down and smiles upon us this day, because we have met as belonging to one family. The best thing in a family is good feeling toward every member of the family. I am proud to become a member of your family—a sister to you all. The sun is your grandfather, and he is the same to me. Your tribe has the distinction of being always very faithful to promises and of possessing great respect and reverence toward sacred things. It is known also that nothing but good feeling prevails in the tribe, and that whenever any member has been found guilty of committing any wrong, that member has been cast out and not allowed to mingle with the other members of the tribe. For all these good qualities in the tribe, you have been chosen as worthy and deserving of all good gifts. I represent the Buffalo tribe, who have sent you this pipe. You are to receive this pipe in the name of all the common people [among the Plains Indians]. Take it, and use it according to my directions. The bowl of the pipe is red stone—a stone not very common and found only at a certain place. This pipe shall be used as a peacemaker. The time will come when you shall cease hostilities against other nations. Whenever peace is agreed upon between two tribes or parties, this pipe shall be a binding instrument. By this pipe the medicine-men shall be called to administer help to the sick."

Turning to the women, she said:

"My dear sisters, the women: You have a hard life to live in this world, yet without you this life would not be what it is. *Wakantanka* intends that you shall bear much sorrow—comfort others in time of sorrow. By your hands the family moves. You have been given the knowledge of making clothing and of feeding the family. *Wakantanka* is with you in your sorrows and joins you in your griefs. He has given you the great gift of kindness toward every living creature on the Earth. You he has chosen to have a feeling for the dead who are gone. He knows that you remember the dead longer than do the men. He knows that you love your children dearly."

Then turning to the children:

"My little brothers and sisters: Your parents were once little children like you, but in the course of time they became men and women. All living creatures were once small, but if no one took care of them they would never grow up. Your parents love you and have made many sacrifices for your sake in order that *Wakantanka* may listen to them and that nothing but good may come to you as you grow up. I have brought this pipe for them, and you shall reap some benefit from it. Learn to respect and reverence this pipe, and above all, lead pure lives. *Wakantanka* is your great grandfather."

Turning to the men:

"Now my dear brothers: In giving you this pipe you are expected to use it for nothing but good purposes. The tribe as a whole shall depend upon it for their necessary needs. You realize that all your necessities of life come from the Earth below, the sky above, and the four winds. Whenever you do anything wrong against these elements, they will always take some revenge upon you. You should reverence them. Offer sacrifices through this pipe. When you are in need of buffalo meat, smoke this pipe and ask for what you need, and it shall be granted you. On you it depends to be a strong help to the women in the raising of children. Share the women's sorrow. *Wakantanka* smiles on the man who has a kind feeling for a woman, because the woman is weak. Take this pipe, and offer it to *Wakantanka* daily. Be good and kind to the little children."

Turning to the chief:

"My older brother: You have been chosen by these people to receive this pipe in the name of the whole Sioux tribe. *Wakantanka* is pleased and glad this day, because you have done what it is required and expected that every good leader should do. By this pipe the tribe shall live. It is your duty to see that this pipe is respected and reverenced. I am proud to be called a sister. May *Wakantanka* look down on us and take pity on us and provide us with what we need. Now we shall smoke the pipe."

Then she took the buffalo chip which lay on the ground, lighted the pipe, and pointing to the sky with the stem of the pipe she said, "I offer this to *Wakantanka* for all the good that comes from above."

(Pointing to the Earth.) "I offer this to the Earth, whence come all good gifts."

(Pointing to the cardinal points.) "I offer this to the four winds, whence come all good things."

Then she took a puff of the pipe, passed it to the chief, and said, "Now my dear brothers and sisters, I have done the work for which I was sent here, and now I will go, but I do not wish any escort. I only ask that the way be cleared before me."

Then rising she started, leaving the pipe with the chief, who ordered that the people be quiet until their sister was out of sight. She came out of the tent on the left side, walking very slowly. As soon as she was outside the entrance, she turned into a white buffalo calf.

> There are no written records to document the time or the place of Sitting Bull's birth. He recalled shifting locations and imprecise dates during his lifetime, probably because memorializing such details lacked significance within the Lakota cosmos. Because non-sedentary people organized their livelihoods around the illumination of the sun, moon, and stars, the passage of an age was measured with little regard to a linear chronology. Moreover, a calendar that dated a series of events using the year 1 CE would have meant nothing to the precontact communities of North America. Differing accounts indicate that Sitting Bull may have been born in 1831, 1832, 1834, or 1837 near the banks of the Missouri River, the Grand River, the Teton River, or the Elk River, which is now known as the Yellowstone River. While encamped near Fort Walsh in the Dominion of Canada, he shared possible facts about his early life. He offered just enough information in the conversations to satisfy the curiosity of the wasi'chus. Among the American visitors to his camp during 1877, journalist Jerome B. Stillson of the New York Herald benefited from the assistance of a stenographer and an interpreter. He captured the translated dialogue word for word with only minor editorial interventions.[2]

I was born on the Missouri River; at least I recollect that somebody told me so—I don't know who told me or where I was told of it.

I am an Uncpapa [Hunkpapa]. Yes; of the great Sioux Nation. My father is dead. My mother lives with me in my lodge.... What I am I am.

I am a man. I see. I know. I began to see when I was not yet born; when I was not in my mother's arms but inside of my mother's belly. It was there that I began to study about my people.

I was still in my mother's insides when I began to study all about my people. God [*Wakantanka*] gave me the power to see out of the womb. I studied there in the womb about many things. I studied about the smallpox that was killing my people—the great sickness that was killing the women and children. I was so interested that I turned over on my side. The God Almighty must have told me at that time that I would be the man to be the judge of all the other Indians—a big man to decide for them in all their ways. I speak. It is enough....

I never taught my people to trust Americans. I have told them the truth—that the Americans are great liars. I have never dealt [or signed a treaty] with the Americans. Why should I? The land belonged to my people. I say I never dealt with them—I mean I never treated [with] them in a way to surrender my people's rights. I traded with them, but I always gave full value for what I got. I never asked the United States government to make me presents of blankets, or cloth, or anything of that kind. The most I did was to ask them to send me an honest trader that I could trade with, and I proposed to give him buffalo robes and elk skins and other hides in exchange for what we wanted. I told every trader who came to our camps that I did not want any favors from him—that I wanted to trade with him fairly and equally, giving him full value for what I got, but the traders wanted me to trade with them on no such terms. They wanted to give little and get much. They told me if I did not accept what they give me in trade they would get the government to fight me. I told them I did not want to fight.

At last, yes, but not until after I had tried hard to prevent a fight. At first my young men, when they began to talk bad, stole five American horses. I took the horses away from them and gave them back to the Americans. It did no good. By and by, we had to fight.

Sitting Bull learned how to speak at a young age, when he began to create lyrical incantations that revealed a keen awareness of the Lakota ways. Drumming often opened a performance until the mood was keyed for the full effect. In the form of poetics, the familiar, colorful stylings addressed subjects such as spirituality, animals, warfare, and nationhood. Accordingly, there were ethnomusicological compositions that punctuated everything from courting to death in the circle of life. Sitting Bull's verses resonated with kith and kin, for they marked important occasions during an individual's maturation in a communal setting. One of his most relatable techniques involved the vocalized imitation of bird sounds, which could be quite captivating to listeners. Audiences expressed delight at his repetition of language in a high, resonant, melodious voice. The variations on ecological themes tended to articulate his shared experiences as well as to accentuate his emotional connections with an ancestral homeland. As commonly practiced by the Siouxan speakers, the rhythms, tonalities, and cadences of hypnotic songs allowed him to find the deepest and broadest sensations of an enchanting soundscape and to represent his coming of age within an oral tradition. His meditations reflected upon a growing self-consciousness, which emerged within the framework of a tribal band.³

[Medicine songs]
Wakantanka,
To him, I am related.
Wakantanka is good.
To him, I am related.
From above a tribe is my friend.
From above an elk is my friend.
From above a man is my friend.

In four places friend,
May you be sacred.
No one is sacred, you said.
In four places friend,
May you be sacred.

[Mother song]
Great Spirit to Earth, he has sent me.
Buffalo for food with, he has sent me.
My mother to Earth was, she sent.
Tribes with her was, she sent.

[Father song]
Alone, alone (to my baby), is loved by everyone.
Alone (to my child), sweet words speak (to everyone).
The little owls, little owls, even them.
Alone, alone, loved by everyone.
Hence alone (to my baby), loved by everyone.

[Bird song]
Pretty bird, you have seen me and took pity on me.
Amongst the tribes to live, you wish for me.
You bird tribes from henceforth, always my relation shall be.

[Wolf song]
Alone in the wilderness I roam.
With much hardship in the wilderness I roam.
A wolf said this to me.

[Thunderbird song]
Against the wind I am coming.
I am seeking the peace pipe.
So, rain I am bringing as I come.

[Fox society song]
You young men, help me, do help me.
My country, I love, so I am doing this.

[Strong Hearts society song]
Friends, whoever runs away [from the enemy]
A woman [he is] they say hence.

Through many discouragements
My life is short.

[Council and chief song]
You tribes, behold me!
The chiefs of old are gone.
Myself, I shall take courage.

Sitting Bull followed the conventions of Plains Indian pictography to celebrate his martial exploits. In gatherings with friends and family, he created visual narratives accompanied by oral expositions. As an indication of skill, he drew memorable feats on cured hides, canvas, or muslin that testified of exceptional prowess. His first coup counting occurred in 1846, as later drawings show mounted chases, horse captures, and hand-to-hand combat. He was identified with a name glyph, an icon of a seated buffalo. His accounts also highlighted a sacred shield, which featured a dark birdlike creature painted on buckskin. Upon initiation into male societies, warriors began to make use of old journals, memorandum books, or regimental rosters to render their deeds as "ledger art." Although uncertainties about origination persist, Four Horns, one of Sitting Bull's uncles, may have copied at least forty items from his nephew's record, including Sitting Bull's coups. One of Sitting Bull's adopted brothers likely added his own works to the assorted collection. James Kimball, an assistant surgeon at Fort Buford, purchased all of them from a Siouxan visitor—possibly a courier. While detained by bluecoats many years later, Sitting Bull told the US Army officers which of the items represented copies of "true scenes" from his life. Eventually, the copies were sent to the Army Medical Museum in Washington DC and handed over to the archives of the Bureau of American Ethnology.[4]

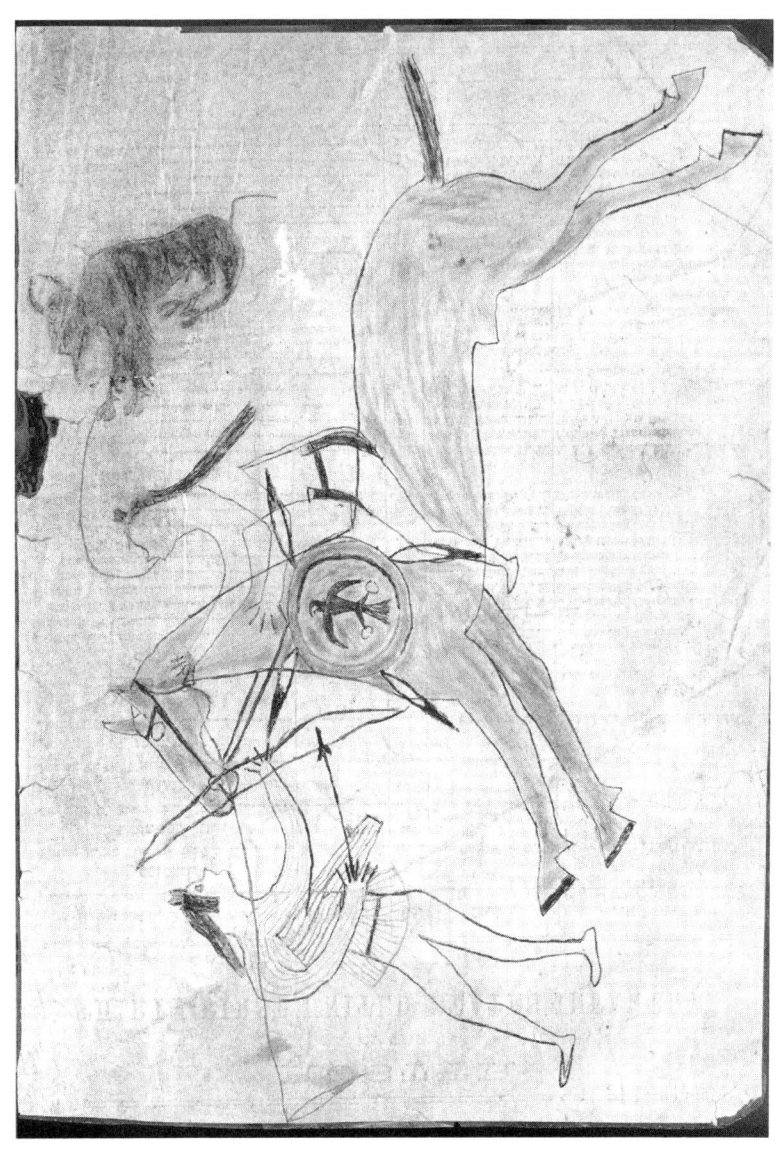

A drawing of war deeds of Sitting Bull and Jumping Bull.

> The terms of the 1851 Fort Laramie Treaty, also known as the Horse Creek Treaty, set the stage for trouble between the United States and the Lakota Sioux. Military commanders insisted that Bear's Rib would speak for the Hunkpapa band thereafter, although he was assassinated by his kinsmen eventually. When Lieutenant Gouverneur K. Warren and his party surveyed the Black Hills, a cohort of chiefs urged the bluecoats to leave the sacred ground without an incident. In the days following September 4, 1857, they met at Bear Butte along the Belle Fourche River. Although Warren did not identify the Lakota by name, Sitting Bull may have delivered a "maiden speech" to mark the occasion. Sitting Bull's encounter with the US Army officer included a rousing message that he reiterated amid peers, that is, the Black Hills must be protected from despoliation by strangers. However, Warren failed to transcribe it verbatim. Walter S. Campbell, a Sitting Bull biographer, later reconstructed it from the retold bits preserved in the oral tradition of Lakota informants. It represented "the first that has come down to us," Campbell concluded to an editor, even if he likely embellished the wording to an extent. His notebooks from the 1920s and 1930s indicated frequent exchanges with Sitting Bull's nephews, One Bull and White Bull.[5]

Friends, the Black Hills belong to me!

Look at me, and look at the Earth. Which is the oldest, do you think? The Earth—and I was born on it. How old is it? I do not know. I will tell you what I think: it is far older than we are. It does not belong to us alone: it was our fathers' and should be our children's after us. When I received it, it was all in one piece, and so I hold it. If the white men take my country, where can I go? I have nowhere to go. I cannot spare it, and I love it very much.

Let us alone. That is what they promised us in their treaty—to let us alone.

What is this white soldier doing here? What did he come for? [He came] to spy out the land and to find a good place for a fort and a road and to dig out gold. He is thinking about the next war, after telling us to make peace with all nations and go to war no more. The white men tell us to make peace, but our enemies will not keep the peace.

We have to make war, and besides, it is our pastime.

This white soldier, this white beard [General William S. Harney], came out here and told us to make peace, to shake all nations by the hand and smoke together. But after he left here he went to war himself, first in the South [against the Seminole of Florida] and now against the Mormons [in the far West]. He says one thing and does another.

Friends, the Black Hills belong to me. The white man must stop here. He must go back.

All we ask is to be let alone. If the Grandfather [or the US president] can control his young men, [then] we shall have peace.

Warfare spread across the northern Great Plains during the 1860s, when the US Army attempted to secure the "Permanent Indian Frontier" near the Missouri River. On July 12, 1864, an eighteen-year-old female named Fanny Kelly was captured during an Oglala raid on a wagon train. The war party traded her to a Hunkpapa named Brings Plenty, who pressured the thin, pale captive into writing messages to non-Indians. She was given the sobriquet "Real Woman." A succession of gift-bearing visitors bargained for her release to no avail. Sitting Bull became interested in her fate, observing the personal hardships around the camp. He sent Crawler, a close confidante, to offer horses to Brings Plenty in exchange for setting her free. As the Strong Hearts society monitored the tense negotiations, his will prevailed after much "jockeying and bluffing." He pitied her and worked to arrange her safe delivery to Fort Sully. Although tall tales about her captivity may have been colorful if not verifiable, she credited his family with providing food, water, and shelter for weeks. "Sitting Bull was a true nobleman," she reminisced later. The encampment averted a serious confrontation during the "Winter When the White Woman Was Rescued." Thus, a Sioux delegation bundled the redeemed captive in buffalo robes and handed her over to the US Army that December.[6]

My friend [Brings Plenty], I sent for this woman to be brought to me at my tent, and you would not give her up. She is not of our ways; her ways are different. And I can see in her face [that] she is homesick, so I send her back....

Why don't you feed her up? Why don't you take better care of her? Traders will be coming. We must take this woman back and make a good showing.

Care for her well. Choose good men to see that no harm comes to her. We can trade on the same trip.

> The Lakota Sioux harassed remote military outposts, yet bows and arrows and single-shot "firesticks" were no match for cannons, pistols, and long-range rifles. During an 1865 military campaign, Brigadier General Alfred Sully filed a report that mentioned Sitting Bull by name for the first time in a direct engagement. A few years later, Major General Philippe Régis Denis de Keredern de Trobriand at Fort Stevenson reported that Sitting Bull was "one of the most dangerous and evil Indians" in the Dakota Territory. Indeed, the paper trails of the day labeled him with various designations such as "chief," "generalissimo," and "medicine man." Endeavoring to secure a large camp that extended over three miles in length, he likely imagined himself to be nothing more or less than a Hunkpapa guardian. Charles Larpenteur, a fur trader on the upper Missouri, kept a diary for his business near Fort Union and transcribed a terse conversation with Sitting Bull in 1867. Although Sitting Bull peacefully participated in the fur trade, he refused to accept annuities and bribes from the government of the United States. He joined a handful of violent raids against the "Long Knives," vowing to avoid negotiating any formal arrangements with the US Army. His standing with the traditional male societies led to greater visibility.[7]

I have killed, robbed, and injured too many white men to believe in a good peace. They are [bad] medicine, and I would eventually die a lingering death. I had rather die on the field of battle—have my skin pierced with bullet holes. And for another thing, I don't want to have anything to do with people who make one carry water on the shoulders and haul manure....

Look at me, see if I am poor, or my people either. The whites may get me at last, as you say, but I will have good times till then. You are fools to make yourselves slaves to a piece of fat bacon, some hardtack, and a little sugar and coffee.

> Sitting Bull's mother, Her Holy Door, began advising him to "hang back" from the wars on the northern Great Plains. His confidence around the campgrounds never waned, but occasional bickering among counterparts distracted him in private. He appeared unflappable to peers. Even in tribal councils, he delighted others by telling a joke or pulling a prank to lighten the mood. His inner circle was accustomed to hearing the sounds of laughter. Frank Grouard, a captive with Polynesian ancestry, found salvation in Sitting Bull's tipi between 1867 and 1871. Likely a deserter from the Montana territorial militia, he sought refuge among roving tribal groups. Although the warriors wanted to kill him, the Hunkpapa decided at a gathering to spare the stranger's life. Sitting Bull, who sometimes spoke in the third person, sat down with the captive. He hoped that an outsider from the "white world" could provide useful information while facilitating multilingual communication. The exchange ended in silence, as Grouard recalled in an interview later that his captors halted their original plans to slay him. Sitting Bull adopted him as another brother, calling him Standing Bear or the Grabber. While quickly gaining fluency in the Siouxan language, he seemed to earn the trust of Sitting Bull.[8]

The coups of Sitting Bull are like the stars, shining and almost numberless. I look; act; I talk afterwards. That which I will is so.

The captive in the Lakota lodge is resting on the robes that Sitting Bull has taken with his own hand from the buffalo, and it is my will that the captive shall not die. When Little Assiniboine [called *Hohe* or Jumping Bull] was taken from his people, it was Sitting Bull who bore him to his lodge and made him his brother. So [too it shall be] with the paleface with the lodge of Sitting Bull this night. He is [now called] Standing Bear, the brother of Sitting Bull.

My will is spoken.

> *The United States sought an end to Red Cloud's War, which was named after a powerful Oglala Lakota chief in the Powder River country. Peace commissioners arrived at Fort Laramie in 1868, when the US Army abandoned the Bozeman Trail and Fort Phil Kearny, Fort C. F. Smith, and Fort Reno. The Indian Office of the Interior Department dispatched Father Pierre-Jean De Smet, a Jesuit missionary, to reach out to Sitting Bull's camp. Charles Galpin, a multilingual trader, and his Sioux wife, Eagle Woman, accompanied the Black Robe on the journey to facilitate communication with aloof figureheads. With a banner image of the Virgin Mary in the vanguard, the entourage included a cadre of Siouxan interpreters. Gathering at Sitting Bull's tipi on June 19, the two-day affair was documented by eyewitnesses. A mass of spectators seated themselves on the ground. Passing a pipe for mutual smoking signified a peaceful coexistence. The councilors agreed that Gall, a Hunkpapa, would travel with the Black Robe to Fort Rice in order to consider the Fort Laramie Treaty. Sitting Bull accepted De Smet's crucifix as a goodwill gesture, but he did not give an endorsement to any document. Even if a few phrases or elaborations may have been interpolated in the handwritten records, the gist of the back-and-forth exchange reappeared in journals over subsequent decades.*[9]

Black Robe, I hardly sustain myself beneath the weight of white men's blood that I have shed. The whites provoked the war; their injustices, their indignities to our families, the cruel, unheard-of, and unprovoked massacre at Fort Lyon of hundreds of Cheyenne women, children, and old men, shook all the veins which bind and support me. I rose, tomahawk in hand, and I have done all the hurt to the whites that I could. Today you are here, and my arms hang to the ground as if dead. I will listen to your good words. And bad as I have been to the white men, just so good I am ready to become toward them. . . .

It sounds good [to talk], but I am satisfied with the old treaty for the hunting tribes if the whites would keep it. Listen, my friend. I have a message for the Grandfather [or the US president]. I do not want anyone to bother my people. I want them to live in peace. I myself have plans for my people, and if they follow my plans, they will never want. They will never hunger. I wish for traders only and no soldiers on my reservation. God [*Wakantanka*] gave us this land, and we are at home here. I will not have my people robbed. We can live if we can keep our Black Hills. We do not want to eat from the hand of the Grandfather. We can feed ourselves....

Father, you pray to the Great Spirit for us. I thank you. I have often besought the kindness of the Great Spirit, but never have I done so more earnestly than today [so] that our words may be heard above and all over the Earth. When I first saw you coming with that flag, my heart beat fast, and I had evil thoughts, caused by the remembrance of the past. I bade my heart be quiet: it was so! And when on the prairie I shook hands with you, and [so did] my cousin and sister, I felt changed and hardly knew what to say. But my heart was glad and quickly scouted deception. I am, and always have been, a fighting fool; my people caused me to be so. They have been troubled and confused by the past: they looked upon their troubles as caused by the whites—and became crazy—and pushed me forward. For the last four years I have led them in bad deeds; the fault is theirs, not mine.

I will now say in their presence: Welcome, Father—the messenger of peace. I hope quiet will again be restored to our country.

As I am not full of words, I will thank you in the hearing of our chiefs and braves, in a sign of peace, hoping you will always wish us well. I have now told you all. All that can be has been said. My people will return [with you] to meet the chiefs of the Grandfather, who wants to make peace with us. I hope it will be done, and whatever is done by others, I will submit to, and for all time to come remain a friend of the whites....

Friends, I have forgotten two things. I wish all to know that I do not propose to sell any part of my country, nor will I have the whites cutting our timber along the rivers, more especially the oak. I am particularly fond of the little groves of oak trees. I love to look at them and feel a reverence for them, because they endure the wintry storms and summer's heat and—not unlike ourselves—seem to thrive and flourish by them. One thing more: those forts filled with white soldiers must be abandoned; there is no greater source of trouble and grievance to my people.

Never had the Lakota named a supreme leader for a greater Sioux nation. Fixed laws of succession or election did not govern the Očhéthi Šakówiŋ, or Seven Council Fires. A spirit of shape-shifting imbued political affairs, because decision-making was decentralized. For the Lakota, "medicine" forged the bonds between authorities and Wakantanka. The word wakan signified something mysterious or incomprehensible, making its efficacy crucial for understanding the loyalty that individuals such as Sitting Bull earned from a populace known for flexibility and adaptation. Though lacking a hereditary title for an administrator of combined bands, he advocated maintaining Lakota unity by avoiding the impositions of the Great Sioux Reservation. Four Horns, a ranking Hunkpapa chieftain, invited senior headmen to a gathering off the reservation, where his nephew Sitting Bull assumed an exalted status in 1868 or so. Crazy Horse, a fearless Oglala, was acknowledged as a subordinate leader. Sitting Bull's oratory for camp management was preserved in a Siouxan dialect, albeit in a partial and fragmentary form. In 1915, Father Eugene Buechel, a Jesuit missionary, linguist, and anthropologist at Rosebud and Pine Ridge, transcribed a recitation from a leadership address and translated it into an English tongue for posterity. Refined over the years, Buechel's linguistic work remains a representative piece of the oral tradition among the Lakota Sioux.[10]

Come now, since this Earth alone remains a long time....

My people, those of you young men close by who grow in heartfelt feelings, be active! These white men are flesh [and] also have hearts. So, like wolves we travel all over the country to prey upon the white men. So, when they quarrel with us, I hunt them down. They have not learned to fight [the Lakota way]. They are like a herd of buffaloes.

It is well now. A little while ago a report was brought that white men are coming. Since I do not want the children to be frightened should they meet them, the families should go move camp downstream. The head warriors will guard you; and sad to say, they will soon bring back word if we shall face them.

My people, since you have declared me first chief today, let us leave here and move camp. Let me select just one site, and there let the children sleep as well as eat. Let us be on our way two days from now.

> Historically, the Lakota developed a rich oral tradition to preserve the cultural values that accentuated their roots of existence. Called ohunkakan, folktales circulated to entertain children around a campfire and to impart knowledge from a long time ago. Through the passing down of lessons, examples, and proverbs from generation to generation, younger Lakota learned from the experiences of their elders and found continuity in changing times. Sitting Bull's grandson, Joseph Fly, remembered forebearers telling wondrous stories of "war with the Crows" during his childhood. His grandfather had prefaced one such story about intertribal rivalries by vowing that he would tell it exactly as it had been told to him long ago. He told of a war party looking for the Crow Indians, who frequently clashed with the Lakota over the hunting grounds west of the Black Hills. He recounted the yarn in a way that bears the hallmarks of Lakota lore, offering an account of "coyote medicine" with a dose of whimsy. It may have suggested an anecdote from an actual event that had been recorded by winter counts around 1870, indicating the survivor skills essential for living in a conflict zone. Perhaps it linked descendants to ancient myths—to a way of life that endures from age to age. One persistent theme is that Sitting Bull's stock of orations abounded with allusions to animals as kindred spirits.[11]

The Sioux were once in camp. They were ready to fight anytime they would hear the words: "Crows are coming!" They had started on the warpath the very night they had camped, so they took their arrows, hatchets, and ropes and started on the trail.

As they were going along silently, they seemed to hear someone singing. They stopped and heard the voice of someone that seemed to be singing behind the hill they were passing, so they went to the spot whence the sounds came from.

When they reached the place where it was, the singer was an old coyote sitting on his hind legs. They went to it, but it never moved from its place. They sat around the coyote and saw that there were some cactus thorns in his feet. They pulled them out for him and stuck some tobacco around the place where the coyote was sitting. They spread a blanket and sat him on the blanket. They painted his tail with red clay and gave it something to eat. Then they began to ask the coyote to help them on the war trail, but he never said a word to them.

Afterward, they went on and left the coyote sitting on the blanket. They went to the Crow's camp and took their best horses and took scalps of some of them and started home.

Next morning, they came to the place where the coyote had been sitting, but it was not there. All that was left was the blanket, which it was sitting on. The things were gone. Then they began to think that the Great Spirit had sent him to help them.

Since that time, the Crows were always beaten in every fight.

PART 2

BATTLEGROUND

Part 2 • Battleground 65

During the early 1870s, Sitting Bull's followers often camped along the banks of the Yellowstone River. Rival tribal groups, not US soldiers, represented his primary adversaries in the locality. One summer day, he shared a vision with a crowd at a campsite. Giving a short incantation, he described a ball of fire blazing through the air. However, it vanished before reaching him. After performing a pipe ceremony, he foresaw an impending battle over the hunting grounds. Two days later, he rode toward the Musselshell River with hundreds of brave companions at his side. A gathering of Flathead Indians loomed ahead. Following a brief skirmish that produced light casualties, the Lakota began to withdraw from the field. Suddenly, Sitting Bull galloped forward to confront a dismounted Flathead. He fought his enemy and was wounded in his left forearm. Whether or not his vision had come to pass, he recovered with more honors. A decade later, his imprisonment at Fort Randall prompted him to draw a pictograph of the incident on foolscap paper. While recording the glories of war deeds, he pointed out the visible scars from battle wounds. His heralded work illustrated typical Plains Indian stylings. The drawings were forwarded by Lieutenant Wallace Tear to Brigadier General John C. Smith, whose son eventually donated them to the Bureau of American Ethnology.[1]

In battle with Flatheads.

The United States wanted to contain the Plains Indians within designated spheres in an effort to reduce intertribal warfare. In 1872, the assistant secretary of the interior, Benjamin R. Cowen, conducted councils with bands of "Tetons" near Fort Peck and learned that Sitting Bull was "the leading man of their people." Other chiefs often deferred to him. However, no one from Washington DC convinced him to join peace talks. Even if he did not intend to commit depredations against the wasi'chus that year, he confirmed plans to fight the Crow Indians all summer long. The Lakota encroachments upon the Crow's turf perpetuated cycles of revenge killings. When Lieutenant Wallace Tear sat down with an imprisoned Sitting Bull at Fort Randall a decade later, the former scribbled notes from a series of conversations with the latter. An interpreter clarified details, particularly Sitting Bull's reminiscences about battling the Crow in the "Land of the Sioux" or a "long way from the Missouri." They included his estimates for the number of warriors engaged and killed, a chronicle of the actions, and a summation of the outcomes. Instead of uttering first-person pronouns, he spoke about himself in a third-person voice. Though animated by memories, he was "diffident" about battles involving the US Army. His record of war deeds was donated eventually to the Bureau of American Ethnology.[2]

Crows [were] always fighting the Sioux. ["Bull"] tried to make friends with them, but they were always doing something bad....

Crows were stealing ponies. ["Bull"] let women go home with presents for Crow chiefs to try and make friends....

The Sioux used to take the Crows prisoners and give them good clothes and feed them up and give them good ponies and then send them back, so they could tell a good story of the Sioux to their people....

Crow Indian [was] killed by "Bull." [An estimated] 200 Sioux ran upon seven Crows hunting in Land of the Sioux and killed them all. Crows had guns. Sioux had nothing but bows and lances. Crows were crossing Missouri [River] a few years ago.

> The Lakota Sioux thrived within an immense living space, but a wave of trespassers began crossing the lands set aside by Red Cloud and the signers of the Fort Laramie Treaty. Off-reservation groups expressed dismay about the presence of US soldiers, who advanced railroad construction across foraging areas and stimulated national interest in the Black Hills. Given the turmoil of the 1870s, a resistance movement spread among the hunters and gatherers of the non-treaty factions. When the councils met in one camp circle or another, their deliberations focused on the defense of ancestral homelands. Lakota governance was highly decentralized, yet thousands of souls began looking to Sitting Bull as their "acknowledged leader" in securing the sacred ground. Time and again, he reiterated the idea of fighting to the last if necessary. Physician Charles A. Eastman, a Santee Sioux with degree credentials from Dartmouth College and Boston University, featured a selection of Siting Bull's oratory in a personalized collection titled Indian Heroes and Great Chieftains (1918). However polished or embroidered for publication later, it was inscribed, Eastman insisted, "as it has been several times repeated to me by men who were present." The internal referencing suggests an original delivery during the spring of 1875, probably at a council on the Powder River.[3]

Behold, my friends, the spring is come; the [maternal] Earth has gladly received the embraces of the [paternal] Sun, and we shall soon see the results of their love! Every seed is awakened and all animal life. It is through this mysterious power that we too have our being, and we therefore yield to our neighbors, even to our animal neighbors, the same right as ourselves to inhabit this vast land.

Yet hear me, friends! We have now to deal with another people, small and feeble when our forefathers first met them but now great and overbearing. Strangely enough, they have a mind to till the soil, and the love of possessions is a disease to them. These people have made many rules that the rich may break but the poor may not! They have a religion in which the poor worship but the rich will not! They even take tithes of the poor and weak to support the rich and those who rule. They claim this mother of ours, the Earth, for their own use and fence their neighbors away from her and deface her with their buildings and their refuse. They compel her to produce out of season, and when sterile she is made to take medicine [called fertilizer] in order to produce again. All this is sacrilege. This nation [called the United States] is like a spring freshet; it overruns its banks and destroys all who are in its path. We cannot dwell side by side. Only seven years ago we made a treaty [at Fort Laramie] by which we were assured that the buffalo country should be left to us forever. Now they threaten to take that from us also. My brothers, shall we submit? Or shall we say to them: First kill me, before you can take possession of my father['s] land!

Amid the Plains Indians, annual pledges of allegiance occurred during the sun dances. The summer ceremonies of 1875 involved sharing a sacred pipe, communing, drumming, fasting, singing, and dancing. In the Montana Territory, Sitting Bull rode a black horse to a friendly gathering of the Hunkpapa, Oglala, Sans Arc, Miniconjou, and Northern Cheyenne. He asked the band leaders to smoke a pipe together at the main lodge, showing that they would cooperate in their common defense. He wore only his breechclout and moccasins. His upper face, arms, legs, and entire body were painted with the holiest color of yellow. The lower part of his face was painted black. A black lightning symbol ran from the corner of one eye over the temple, across his forehead, and ended with the other eye. He started to circle around the "medicine pole," making gesticulations as if he were battling invisible enemies. A multitude joined with him in a celebration. His performance helped to inspire the young and old alike. Although remembrances of the council proceedings remained sketchy, he insisted that Wakantanka had given him a special responsibility to protect the women and children of his community. Many years later, translators at a military outpost helped a visiting journalist obtain Sitting Bull's recollections of what happened before the Great Sioux War.[4]

I need not tell you how we have been deceived by the white people, for if you are friendly you know the facts, and if you are our enemy you would not believe me. The Black Hills country was set aside for us by the government; it was ours by solemn agreement, and we made the country our home. We realized how our lands had been taken, our reservations circumscribed, my people driven like so many wild beasts toward a common center to be shot down by encircling soldiery. Our homes in the Black Hills were invaded when gold was discovered there; we asked for protection, which was promised, but with all our importunities the government refused to come to our aid. White thieves committed depredations and then accused my people of perpetrating the acts. Well, it is no use to tell you more....

It is our belief that we can only come into the presence of the Great Spirit through sufferings of the flesh, but though the ceremony indicates pain to those who participate, yet there is really no suffering when there is an acceptance. At the conclusion of the third day of our dance, I became unconscious of my material surroundings and was awakened in the spirit before the Great Ruler [*Wakantanka*]. He smoked [tobacco in the ceremony] and then gave to me the peace pipe; we were seated together in a beautiful tipi, and after smoking, he said to me, "*Tatáŋka Íyotake*, you are being surrounded by your enemies; in seven suns you will be attacked by your ancient foe, the Crow Indians, but over these I will give you a victory; three more suns shall not set before your people will have an engagement with white soldiers; the fight will be a terrible one, but your enemies will be slaughtered, and you shall have a great victory. This prophecy you can make to your people, for they are weary, and this will give them courage."

After thus speaking the Great Spirit vanished, and sometime during the night I recovered consciousness. I prophesied to my people as the Great Spirit directed, and [they saw] that it came to pass as I uttered. My people are the witnesses [of its fulfillment].

> A number of the Lakota harassed mining parties and wagon trains on the roads around the Black Hills, which resulted in public outrage as far away as Washington DC. US President Ulysses S. Grant wanted the War Department to send additional troops to protect Americans, because he knew that the discovery of gold would generate frequent clashes with the Plains Indians. Congress appointed William Allison, a Republican senator from Iowa, to chair a new peace commission, which endeavored in 1875 to extinguish Lakota title to millions of acres. Whereas altering the Fort Laramie Treaty required signatures from three-fourths of all Lakota males, the Allison commission failed to gain concessions for the acquisition of the real estate. The chiefs at the agencies, including Red Cloud, rejected the heavy-handed overtures. Though invited to the Red Cloud agency, Sitting Bull and Crazy Horse flatly refused the official summons. The former sent word through a multilingual messenger named Louis Richaud, who passed along the Lakota's repudiation of the governmental ploy in plain English. Captain Gregory Bourke, an aid to the commander of the Department of the Platte, Brigadier General George Crook, noted for the record that Sitting Bull communicated in the "haughtiest manner." Simply put, Sitting Bull indicated that the Black Hills were not for sale.[5]

Are you the Great God [Wakantanka] that made me, or was it the Great God that made me who sent you?

If he asks me to come see him, I will go, but the Big Chief of the white men must come see me. I will not go to the reservation. I have no land to sell.

There is plenty of game here [to the west of the Black Hills] for us. We have enough ammunition. We don't want any white men here.

By 1876, the Grant administration had concluded that the Lakota would never give up their legal right to the Black Hills without a fight. Federal agents received instructions to send runners to the winter camps ordering them to the reservation by January 31. If any did not heed the order, then the US Army's centennial campaign would strike the "hostiles" in the hunting grounds. Sitting Bull's followers encamped on the Yellowstone River near the mouth of the Powder River, where they planned to raid Crow and Arikara villages. Relocating to the valley of the Little Bighorn River that spring, Lakota, Cheyenne, and Arapaho lodges assembled upon what they knew to be the Greasy Grass. Their scouts fanned out from the valley, looking for signs of game. In the wake of a sun dance, Sitting Bull warned the assemblage about a pending onslaught by US soldiers. On June 17, a cohort of Plains Indian warriors repelled a large military column in the Battle of the Rosebud. A week later, Sitting Bull climbed a hilltop east of the Little Bighorn, carrying with him offerings of tobacco, a sacred pipe, and a buffalo robe for Wakantanka. He uttered a "dreamy cry" in the presence of One Bull, his nephew. Consequently, the Battle of the Little Bighorn erupted soon after his prayers ended.[6]

> *Wakantanka*, pity me.
> In the name of the tribe, I offer you this peace pipe.
> Wherever the sun, the moon, the earth, the four points of the winds, there you are always.
> Father, save the tribe. I beg you. Pity me.
> We wish to live. Guard us against all misfortunes or calamities.
> Pity me.

Even though the War Department planned and coordinated the centennial campaign, military commanders did not expect to meet a large opposing force during the Great Sioux War. The main camp of the Lakota, Cheyenne, and Arapaho fought the Seventh Cavalry in the Battle of the Little Bighorn, killing the men in uniform under Lieutenant Colonel George Armstrong Custer's direct command. Meanwhile, a handful of shattered companies survived a siege on a nearby hill until reinforcements under Brigadier General Alfred H. Terry arrived. When the eagle bone whistles sounded on June 25, 1876, Sitting Bull looked after the women, children, and elderly among the Hunkpapa band. He guided them to safety on the far western side of the valley beyond the cavalrymen's reach. He urged those entering the fray not to rob or to disturb the fallen enemies, yet the pilfering, stripping, and mutilating of corpses did occur. Even if he did not participate in the hand-to-hand fighting across the Greasy Grass, his steadfastness enabled thousands to rush bravely into the combat zone. They had not sought the confrontation but had been well-prepared for it. They exhibited fierce determination to defend their families and friends. A year later, the New York Herald published a battlefield map "partly suggested and corrected by Chief Sitting Bull." A military cartographer arranged its visualizations.[7]

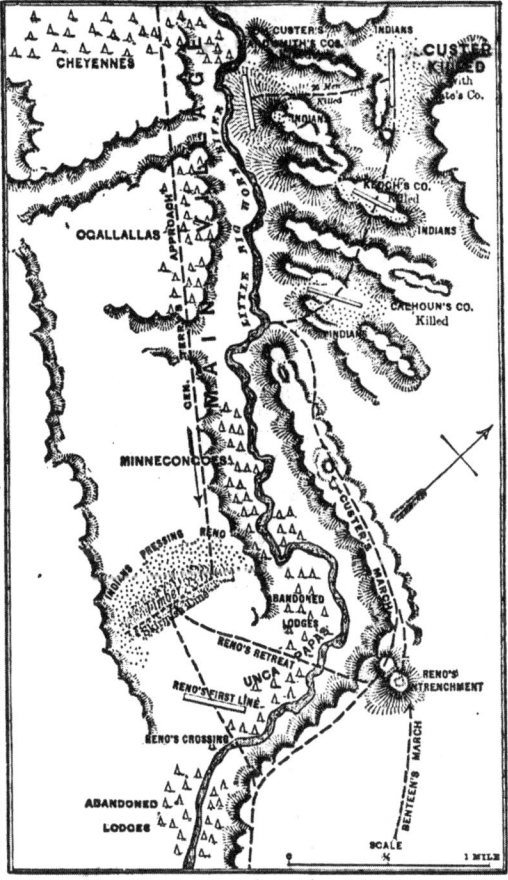

A Map Partly Suggested and Corrected by Chief Sitting Bull, *New York Herald*, November 16, 1877.

Sitting Bull clearly remembered the Battle of the Little Bighorn, but he later offered only brief and evasive statements about what happened from June 25 to June 26, 1876. Knowing that the dramatic event evoked strong emotions, he preferred to avoid enflaming the passions of the wasi'chus *whenever they interrogated him. Unfortunately, creative writers all over the United States fabricated accounts about his role in the Great Sioux War. For example, some averred incorrectly that he killed Lieutenant Colonel George Armstrong Custer with his own hands. A few dubbed him a Napoleonic genius, who supposedly attended the US Military Academy at West Point. He chafed at the erroneous allegations of cowardice, which insinuated that he stayed safe in his tipi or hid with the women, children, and elderly in camp. Whenever disputing the falsehoods, misrepresentations, and hoaxes, he lamented the "strange lies." He endeavored to set the record straight. Upon finding sanctuary in the Dominion of Canada in 1877, he agreed to sit for an interview with journalist Jerome B. Stillson. Major James M. Walsh of the North-West Mounted Police sat alongside interpreters to moderate. The* New York Herald *printed the translated dialogue word for word, revealing the maneuvers on "Custer's last battlefield." With a handful of possible interpolations, it was edited for a non-Indian audience.*[8]

I am no chief. I am a man. No. I am nothing—neither a chief nor a soldier. Nothing.

Oh, I used to be a kind of a chief; but the Americans made me go away from my father's hunting ground. Your people look up to men because they are rich; because they have much land, many lodges, many squaws? Well, I suppose my people look up to me because I am poor. That is the difference....

We know that on the other side [of the border] the buffaloes will not last very long. Why? Because the country there is poisoned with blood—a poison that kills all the buffaloes or drives them away. It is strange that the Americans should complain that the Indians kill buffaloes. We kill buffaloes, as we kill other animals for food and clothing and to make our lodges warm. They kill buffaloes—for what? Go through your country. See the thousands of carcasses rotting on the plains. Your young men shoot for pleasure. All they take from a dead buffalo is his tail, or his head, or his horns, perhaps, to show they have killed a buffalo. What is this? Is it robbery? You call us savages. What are they? The buffaloes have come north. We have come north to find them and to get away from a place where the people tell lies....

    It is well. We thought we were whipped. Not at first; but by and by, yes. Afterwards, no. Here (pointing to Major Marcus A. Reno's crossing on the map). It was some two hours past the time when the sun is in the center of the sky. The Long Hair [Lieutenant Colonel George Armstrong Custer came to the Greasy Grass]. The Long Hair commanded. I have said that I never saw him. Not here, but there. A chief leads his warriors.

    It was so. I was lying in my lodge. Some young men ran into me and said: "The Long Hair is in the camp. Get up. They are firing in the camp." I said, all right, and jumped up and stepped out of my lodge. Here, with my people (designated as "abandoned lodges" on the map). Yes. The old men, the squaws, and the children were hurried away. Yes. Some of the Miniconjou women and children also left their lodges when the attack began. Yes, the fighting men. Oh, we fell back, but it was not what warriors call a retreat; it was to gain time. It was the Long Hair who retreated. My people fought him here in the brush (designating the timber behind which the Indians pressed Reno) and he fell back across here (placing his finger on the line of Reno's retreat to the bluffs). Of course. Not then; not there. Why, down here (Sitting Bull indicated with his finger the place where Custer approached and touched the river). That was where the big fight was fought a little later. After the Long Hair was driven back to the bluffs, he took this road (tracing with his finger the line of Custer's march on the map) and went down to see if he could not beat us there.

    Hell! I mean a thousand devils [were fighting]. The squaws were like flying birds; the bullets were like humming bees. They ran back again to the right, here and there (the place where the words "abandoned lodges" are). They ran to the fight—the big fight. Yes. You have forgotten. You forget that only a few soldiers were left by the Long Hair on those bluffs. He took the main body of his soldiers with him to make the big fight down here on the left. I have spoken. It is enough. The squaws could deal with them. There were none but squaws and papooses in front of them that afternoon. They fought. Many young men are missing from our lodges. But is there an

American squaw, who has her husband left? Were there any Americans left to tell the story of that day? No.

I have heard that there are trees which tremble. Yes. Hah! A great white chief, whom I met once, spoke these words, Silver Aspens, trees that shake; those were the Long Hair's soldiers. They were brave men. They were tired. They were too tired.

Your people were killed. I tell no lies about dead men. These men who came with the Long Hair were as good men as ever fought. When they rode up their horses were tired, and they were tired. When they got off from their horses, they could not stand firmly on their feet. They swayed to and fro—so my young men have told me—like the limbs of cypresses in a great wind. Some of them staggered under the weight of their guns. But they began to fight at once; but by this time, as I have said, our camps were aroused, and there were plenty of warriors to meet them. They fired with needle guns. We replied with magazine guns—repeating rifles. It was so (and here Sitting Bull illustrated by patting his palms together with the rapidity of a fusillade). Our young men rained lead across the river and drove the white braves back. And then they rushed across themselves. And then they found that they had a good deal to do. There was so much doubt about it that I started down there (here again, pointing to the map) to tell the squaws to pack up the lodges and get ready to move away....

I have heard of it from the warriors. At first they did [advance], but afterward they found it better to try and get around him [the Long Hair]. They formed themselves on all sides of him, except just at his back. As long as it takes the sun to travel from here to here (indicating some marks upon his arm, with which, apparently, he used to gauge the progress of the shadow of his lodge across his arm, and probably meaning half an hour).

The trouble was with the soldiers [on the battleground]. They were so exhausted and their horses bothered them so much that they could not take good aim. Some of their horses broke away from them and left them to stand and drop and die. When the Long Hair, the General, found that he was so outnumbered and threatened on his flanks, he took the best course he could have taken. The bugle blew. It was an order to fall back. All the men fell back, fighting and dropping. They could not fire fast enough, though. But from our side it was so (here he clapped his hands rapidly, twice a second, to express with what quickness and continuance the balls flew from the Henry and Winchester rifles wielded by the Indians). They could not stand up under such a fire. They kept in pretty good order. Some great chief must have commanded them all the while. They would fall back across a coulee and make a fresh stand beyond on higher ground. The map is pretty nearly right. It shows where the white men stopped and fought before they were all killed. I think that is right—down there to the left, just above the Little Bighorn [River]. There was one party driven out there, away from the rest, and there a great many men were killed. The places marked on the map are pretty nearly the places where all were killed. Every man [fought], so far as my people could see. There were no cowards on either side. The sun was there (pointing to within two hours from the western horizon). [The battle continued] through most of the going forward of the sun.

I have talked with my people; I cannot find one who saw the Long Hair until just before he died. He did not wear his hair long as he used to wear it. His hair was like yours. It was short, but it was of the color of the grass when the frost comes. . . .

Well, I have understood that there were a great many brave men in that fight, and that from time to time, while it was going on, they were shot down like pigs. They could not help themselves. One by one, the officers fell. I believe the Long Hair rode across once from this place down here (showing the place where others were killed) to this place up here (indicating the spot on the map where Custer fell), but I am not sure about this. Anyway, it was said that up there where the last fight took place, where the last stand was made, the Long Hair stood like a sheaf of corn with all the ears fallen around him. . . .

All this was far up on the bluffs, far away from the Sioux encampments. I did not see it. It is told to me. But it is true. No. My people did not want his scalp. I have said: he was a great chief.

At one time, as I have told you, I started down to tell the squaws to strike the lodges. I was then on my way up to the right end of the camp, where the first attack was made on us. But before I reached that end of the camp where the Miniconjou and Uncpapa [Hunkpapa] squaws and children were, and where some of the other squaws—Cheyennes and Oglalas—had gone, I was overtaken by one of the young warriors who had just come down from the fight. He called out to me. He said: "No use to leave camp; every white man is killed." So, I stopped and went no further. I turned back, and by and by, I met the warriors returning....

I have said enough.

Part 2 • Battleground　　　　　　　　　　　　　　　　81

> The press corps across the country propagated harrowing accounts of the US Army's defeat at the Little Bighorn River, but few delivered accurate coverage of Sitting Bull's role. Even though telegraph wires quickened the spread of news, much of what happened on the battleground remained clouded by misinformation. Millions of Americans read the sensational headlines about the centennial campaign and expected the War Department to swiftly punish the Plains Indians for the "Custer Massacre." At nightfall on June 26, 1876, the tribal groups along the Greasy Grass scattered. Before hitting the trail, Sitting Bull rode through the valley to see the carnage. He felt satisfaction that his vision came to pass, as the fighting appeared to culminate at the very spot of his tobacco offering. He also experienced great sadness, because so many people failed to heed his words of warning. He dismounted, filled his pipe, and closed his eyes. He prayed for the dead, including one of his own children—a victim of a horse-hoof accident in the chaos. He asked Wakantanka to receive the spirits of the warriors, who had fought with honor. A reporter from St. Louis, Missouri, caught up with him many years later and transcribed his reflections on the day after with help from translators at Fort Yates.[9]

I was not in the fight and know nothing about it, save what my warriors have told me. . . .

Now it is asked, why do I refuse to talk about our fight with [Lieutenant Colonel George Armstrong] Custer? You cannot wonder at my silence. Every man's rifle is leveled at the Indian's heart; every white man cries out: "Let us avenge Custer," and a special hatred is directed against Sitting Bull. I am afraid to trust myself away from my people. They have tempted me with large offers to travel in the [United] States, but the [railroad] cars would make me sick, and once wholly within their power, the white people would starve me to death, because they say I murdered Custer. . . .

On the night after the battle, our tents were struck and we started northward, expecting an attack on the following day. My warriors were very tired, and had the pursuit been an active one we would, no doubt, have been overcome. Had not [Captain Frederick W.] Benteen joined forces with [Major Marcus A.] Reno when we had the latter surrounded in the woods, there would have been few soldiers left in the three commands to tell the story of their disaster.

No one can tell who killed Custer. It is impossible because of two facts: first, none of my braves knew Custer, and, second, the tumult and smoke of the battle were so great that combatants were often obscured entirely. The fighting was therefore promiscuous. None of my people ever boasted to me that they had killed Custer.

I have now told you all that I know in regard to the fight with Custer. I can't see why the white people hold me responsible for his death; the soldiers attacked us, and we fought to defend ourselves. If all my people had been slaughtered, the whites would have been glad.

> As the Great Sioux War continued to unfold, Sitting Bull sent messengers to the various Lakota agencies. If the "rascality" about the Black Hills came to an end, he announced, then he would counsel anyone off the Great Sioux Reservation to make peace with the United States. After the death of "Long Hair," however, the wasi'chus demanded retribution. The non-treaty Indians split up into smaller bands to search for game. Factionalism abounded for the rest of the long, hot summer. Although some wanted to beg for government-issued rations, others preferred to follow the buffalo herds until the colder weather arrived. On August 29, 1876, several chiefs from the Oglala, Miniconjou, Brule, Sans Arc, and other Sioux bands encamped at a creek near the head of the Powder River. They dispatched three couriers after a council to deliver the "sentiment of Sitting Bull" to the Standing Rock agency, where Lieutenant Colonel W. P. Carlin of the Seventeenth Infantry held command. They chose a Hunkpapa curiously named Man That Smells His Hand to speak with military authorities, repeating that Sitting Bull had communicated the exact words for him to say. In effect, it was a "Plains Indian telegram." The US Army officer transcribed the courier's message for the record on September 6, 1876.[10]

This land belongs to us. It is a gift to us from the Great Spirit. The Great Spirit gave us the game in this country. It is our privilege to hunt the game in our country.

The white man came here to take the country from us by force. He has brought misery and wretchedness into our country. We were here killing game and eating, and all of a sudden [this summer] we were attacked by white men [in the armed forces]. You will now depart and return to Standing Rock [agency]. Tell the commanding officer that we are tired of fighting and that we want the soldiers to stop fighting us. Tell him to repeat these words to the Great Father [or the US president]: The Great Spirit above us gave us this country. It is ours [by the will of *Wakantanka*], and He is looking down on us today. He sees the bloody deeds going on in this country. Though He gave us the country, He did not give us the right to dispose of it. It is our duty to defend our country. We did not say to the white man "come out and fight us." We did not ask them to come out at all. We did not want to fight them; but now if they wish to withdraw they may. We do not wish to fight them....

Perhaps the whites think they can exterminate us, but God, the Great Spirit, will not permit it.

Throughout the rest of 1876, the United States deployed more and more troops to the Black Hills area in pursuit of the Lakota and other "hostiles." Sitting Bull evaded them by moving his camp along the Little Missouri River to Killdeer Mountain. Following the Moon When Plums Are Ripe, he observed a group of bluecoats and warriors exchanging gunfire at a geological formation known as Slim Buttes on September 9. A month later, his camp headed to the northwest for another buffalo hunt. He brought along a "private secretary" named John Bruguier, a former agency interpreter who dressed like a cowboy but spoke like a Sioux. Called "Big Leggings," he scribbled a message from Sitting Bull upon a piece of paper. It was impaled on a stick in the middle of a road, where a military wagon train was transporting supplies on October 16. Among the troopers on escort duty, Lieutenant Colonel Elwell S. Otis read it and responded with his own note. Accordingly, Sitting Bull's surrogates rode forward to speak with Otis. They repeated prior admonishments with regard to the hunting grounds, adding that they were hungry and needed ammunition. They asked for peace, not war. The US Army officer preferred to avoid a clash, leaving 150 pounds of hard bread and two sides of bacon for them.[11]

I want to know what you are doing traveling on this road. You scare all the buffalo away. I want to hunt on the place. I want you to turn back from here. If you don't [leave], I will fight you again. I want you to leave what you have got here and turn back from here.

I am your friend, Sitting Bull.

I mean [to have] all the rations you have got and some powder. Wish you would write as soon as you can.

> Nicknamed "Man with the Bear Coat," Colonel Nelson A. Miles assembled a large military column on the Tongue River to hunt for Sitting Bull. The latter agreed to meet the former at Cedar Creek, where two days of talks began on October 20, 1876. Under a white flag, the rivals faced one another and shook hands for the first time. The US Army officer deliberately studied the renowned Lakota, who seemed "courteous" but unyielding in his defense of the Black Hills. "I'll fight and die fighting before any white man can make me an agency Indian," Sitting Bull repeated to Miles. The standoff reached an impasse on the second day, as the opposing parties returned to their separate lines. Both sides dreaded the prospect of a long, cold winter, which portended month after month of hard fighting. As the two parleyed, neither could speak the other's language with fluency. Whatever they said, much was lost in translation. Even though "Big Leggings" was hired by the colonel to interpret for them, no contemporary transcription by the chief's "private secretary" has survived. A half-century later, Sitting Bull's nephew White Bull relayed his uncle's rendition of the Cedar Creek affair to Walter S. Campbell, who jotted it down with the help of a Sioux interpreter named Sam Eagle Chasing.[12]

My friends, I own this country. I will always be here, but you [soldiers] just come out to look for me. When you find me, you start to fight [against] me. That is what I do not want.

All my Indians live in this country with wild game. That is all they live on. They are stronger and healthier. That is all I am looking after—to see my Indians get along. God [*Wakantanka*] created this world for me and also the game and the Black Hills. He gave it to me. So, I claim that this is my country. So, I do not want any of your white people to come in this country and bother my Indians. I use the buffalo hide for a blanket, for a moccasin, for leggings, to make tents out of, and [to] make bags to carry my food in. Also, I make the ropes out of it to catch all my horses. Also, I make a wooden saddle and cover it with buffalo hide. I make my strings out of it.

The Black Hills were full of [potential] money—full of minerals, a lot of trees, and all kinds of good soil and water—and I know all this belongs to my Indians for a future time. As long as my Indians [are] living on this country, they get the benefit out of these Black Hills. But the government and all of the high officers were figuring and scheming of ways to get the Black Hills. . . .

Every time, I like to see a white man. I like to be friendly. I do not want to fight if I do not have to [fight]. All I look out for is to see how and where [there is] more meat for my people and more animals for my people. I look out for what God has got for me to eat. Any white man comes out in my country for post trader and for merchant, I always try to go there and trade back and forth as best as I know how.

There is more buffalo here. That is what I came here to get now [in order] to feed my people. Yes, I made a hunt twice now. I eat well. After I crossed the Yellowstone [River] to hunt buffalo, a bunch of government soldiers scared away buffalo. When I met them, they started shooting and have [caused] a little fight just a while ago. And I know you come here again to fight me and that all you are made for [is] to fight.

Your boys are lining up first, so I lined up mine last. I do not like to start a fight, but lining up your soldiers [is a] sign that you want to fight me again. Therefore, I lined up my Indians to be ready. You are the man that lined up first. You close up your line first; then, I [will] close up mine. High Bear (speaking as an aside), bunch up the Indians again where they started from.

I have not had enough meat. I will make another hunt. Then, I will know where to go. . . .

No. That is the bunch I am trying to protect, the young and old. I would not give up any, and I hunt so they will have enough meat. When I have enough, I will cross over the Missouri [River], where I crossed before at the same old crossover. After I gather up a lot of meat and when I think I have enough to carry me through, I will go right straight back to the Black Hills. I will winter there. In the Black Hills, where a creek called Cottonwood flows into a creek called Spearfish, [there] is a place called Water Hole. And there are other Indians. So, they will pick out their own place in the Black Hills, and where it is suitable to have agencies, [all my Indians] will live in the Black Hills.

Yes, if you come along, give me some ammunition, bullets, and powder. After I have my meat for my people, then I will come back.

You are telling a lot of lies. We had talks yesterday. I agreed with you on everything, [and at that time] so did you agree with me on everything I said. But now today, you are changed. . . .

Now the talks [must] be over. You are getting mad. Your soldiers are preparing for a fight again. Let us dismiss the council.

PART 3

BORDER CROSSINGS

The spring thaw of 1877 permitted Sitting Bull and his followers to enter the "Grandmother's Land"—an allusion to British Queen Victoria and the Dominion of Canada. Although a steady stream of Lakota families returned to the Great Sioux Reservation, Sitting Bull led an exodus across the northern border of the United States. Refugees took a crooked path along the White Mud River as far as Frenchmen's Creek, which flowed on the western side of Wood Mountain. Near Pinto Horse Butte, Major James M. Walsh of the North-West Mounted Police gave them a stern admonition: the "Great White Mother" would provide asylum only if her laws were obeyed. By May 26, at least 135 lodges had encamped some sixty miles north of the international boundary line. Abbot Martin Marty, a Benedictine missionary assigned to one of the federal Indian agencies in the United States, visited the refugee camp in Canada. Accompanied by an agency interpreter, a military scout, and Siouxan escorts, Marty met with Sitting Bull for eight days. They discussed seeking a resolution with the US Army, but the Lakota leader wondered: "Why did you wait until half my people were killed before you came?" Marty's abridged version of the meeting appeared in the Annals of Catholic Missions of America *the next year.*[1]

You come from America, but you are a priest and welcome [to meet with us]. The priest harms no man, and we will give him food and protection and listen to his words.

I hate the Americans, because they persecute us. They drive us from our lands and give them to white settlers. They shoot our squaws, and because we fight to defend them, they send soldiers to kill us or make us prisoners and put us on reservations; after which, they refuse to give us ammunition, take our guns, and fail to supply us with food. Indians have hunted all their lives, and they do not want to give up the chase [of prey]. They live upon game; but they cannot get game if you take their guns away. We bought our guns, and we bought our powder and shot. We gave robes and the skins of elks for these things, and they belong to us as much as those of the whites belong to them. The English will let us keep our guns and ammunition, and we can live in peace here [in Canada]. If we go back [to the United

States], we will be driven like dogs, the young men will be killed, and the old men and squaws starved to death.

This is our friend—a good man and a priest, who has come far to tell us what to do. We want you to tell him if the English are willing for us to stay on their soil.

> Given the presence of game between the Cypress Hills and Wood Mountain, Sitting Bull decided to remain in the Dominion of Canada. His coalition to defend the Black Hills had fallen apart, which left him in a state of uneasiness. While he assessed the situation north of the 49th parallel, the North-West Mounted Police kept a close watch on the refugees encamped near Fort Walsh. Meanwhile, the Hayes administration organized a commission to persuade Sitting Bull and the free Lakota to surrender to the United States. Headed by Brigadier General Alfred H. Terry, the commissioners arrived at the Canadian outpost on October 15, 1877. Commissioner of the North-West Mounted Police, Lieutenant Colonel James F. Macleod, greeted them and organized a council. Two days later, US Army officers, diplomats, scouts, stenographers, interpreters, journalists, and many others gathered in a large room. General Terry, who was nicknamed "One Star," sat in a chair, while Sitting Bull and an entourage assumed their positions upon assorted buffalo robes. Skipping a traditional pipe ceremony, the Americans spoke about governmental requirements for peace. "It is time for bloodshed to cease," General Terry concluded. Afterward, Sitting Bull rose to speak. As interpreters tried to make sense of the spellbinding words, he brushed aside "One Star." Thus, the council ended.[2]

For sixty-four years you have kept me and my people [south of the 49th parallel] and treated us bad. What have we done that you should want us to stop? We have done nothing. It is all the people on your side that have started us to do all these depredations.

We could not go anywhere else, and so we took refuge in this country. It was on this side of the country we learned to shoot, and that is the reason why I came back to it again. I would like to know why you came here.

In the first place, I did not give you the country, but you followed me from one place to another, so I had to leave and come over to this country. I was born and raised in this country with the Red River Half-Breeds [or Métis], and I intend to stop with them. I was raised hand in hand with the Red River Half-Breeds, and we are going to that part of the country, and that is the reason why I have come over here. (He shakes hands with British officers.) That is the way I was raised in the hands of these people here, and that is the way I intend to be with them.

You have got ears [to hear], and you have got eyes to see with them, and you see how I live with these people. You see me? Here I am! If you think I am a fool, [then] you are a bigger fool than I am. This house is a medicine-house. You come here to tell us lies, but we don't want to hear them. I don't wish any such language used to me, that is, to tell me such lies in my Great Mother's house [a Canadian outpost]. Don't you say two more words. Go back home where you came from. This country is mine, and I intend to stay here and to raise this country full of grown people. See these people here. We were raised with them. (Again, he shakes hands with British officers.)

That is enough; so, no more. You see me shaking hands with these people. The part of the country you gave me [for hunting] you ran me out of. I have now come here to stay with these people, and I intend to stay here. I wish you to go back and to "take it easy" going back. (He takes a Santee Sioux Indian by the hand.)

These Santees—I was born and raised with them. He is [my kinsman and is] going to tell you something about them....

I could tell you more, but that is all I have to tell you. If we told you more—why, you would not pay any attention to it. That is all I have to say. This part of the country does not belong to your people. You belong on the other side; this side belongs to us.

With each passing day in Canada, the plight of the free Lakota worsened. Sitting Bull sent messages to various tribal groups near Wood Mountain, asking their leaders to consider forming a pan-Indian confederation. He accompanied hunting parties along the 49th parallel to search for game, but most returned to Pinto Horse Butte empty-handed. He embraced a group of Nez Percé Indians escaping from the US Army during 1877. He met with White Bird, a Nez Percé war chief, who became a kindred spirit in exile. Rumors abounded that Sitting Bull planned to instigate a border war against the Americans, although he vowed to friends—echoing the famous words of a Nez Percé leader—to "fight no more forever." He directed an emissary to petition the Canadian government for provisions, seeds, and tools. Perhaps the "Grandmother" would grant a parcel of land to till, or so he hoped. "My arrows are broken," he lamented, "and I have thrown my warpaint to the winds." While contemplating raids against the Crow Indians, he decided to meet with Major James M. Walsh at Wood Mountain on March 23, 1879. In addition to his family members, a few headmen of the Hunkpapa and Miniconjou joined the council. Seeking a kind of middle ground, Sitting Bull promised to not prevent anyone in his camp from returning to the United States if they desired.[3]

What I wish to say to the Grandmother [or British Queen Victoria] is I have but one heart, and it is the same today as when I first shook your hand. When I first entered her country [in Canada], I told you that my heart was pale at how my people had been persecuted by the Americans, and that I came to the Grandmother's country to sleep sound and ask her to have pity on me—that I never would again shake the hand of an American. I went at your request to the Grandmother's fort to meet the Americans, but I will never meet them again....

I am looking to the north for my life and hope the Grandmother will never ask me to look to the country I left, although mine; and not even the dust of it did I sell, but the Americans can have it [while I am here]. I never look at the Grandmother's children with a side face. I told you before, and I tell you now, I am never going to leave the Grandmother's country.

I see many roads coming; they are the Grandmother's [roads]. I will live with them. Those who wish to return to the Americans can go, and those who wish to remain here, if the Grandmother wishes to give them a piece of land, can farm. But I will remain what I am until I die, a hunter, and when there are not buffalo or other game, I will send my children to hunt and live on prairie mice, for when an Indian is shut up in one place his body becomes weak....

You have for many months been advising us to think of getting our living from the ground. Will you tell me where we will find this ground?

As the bison herd near Wood Mountain dissipated, Sitting Bull and his followers hunted southward across the international border in search of "something for my children to eat." *Correspondent Stanley Huntley of the* Chicago Tribune *caught up with him near Rock Creek, bringing along an interpreter to help facilitate an interview on June 16, 1879. Although portions of what appeared in print may have been sensationalized, he reportedly found the last* blotáhunka *outfitted with blue leggings, beaded moccasins, a skin shirt, and a blanket drawn loosely around his waist. At an isolated campsite, Long Dog, Pretty Bear, One Bull, Bear's Cap, Big Road, and other members of the hunting party observed Huntley's face-to-face chat with Sitting Bull. What emerged from the close encounter was a journalistic account that revealed the other side of the Plains Indian wars to an American audience. With scribbled notes in hand, Huntley dashed to Fort Buford to dispatch a long telegram to an editor. Other correspondents attempted but failed to obtain an audience with the free Lakota, prompting some to allege that Huntley's interview was a fabrication. Despite the popular appeal of fake news, the sympathetic treatment of Sitting Bull challenged many of the negative stereotypes in print at the time.*[4]

You are an American. What do you want? You are a spy.

How do I know you will tell your people the truth? You have said that your brothers tell stories about me, and my people say they say we have killed the white men and stolen horses. These stories are lies. I will tell my people what you say to me and no more. If you tell me the truth, [then] I will tell them the truth. If you don't tell me the truth, then what I tell them will be lies. I have not killed the whites. I have not stolen their horses, but your people sent the Long Knives against me. Why do you do that?

I hate them. Do you ask me why? Because I and my people have always been deceived by them. They asked us to go to the gift-houses [at the federal Indian agencies] and said they would care for us and feed us. Many of my people went. They believed what the Americans said to them. They were there but a short time, and then they were told they must farm. Some of them would not do this. Then they found their rations were short.

It is not many years ago your people said they would give us the country of the Black Hills. They said our children should have it and own it for them [and] that it should be our hunting ground. As soon as they found there was shining dust there, they drove us from it, and told us the country did not belong to us. Such actions make me so [mad] that I cannot believe them. We went away from there peacefully, though we know it was rich with gold, for the sake of peace to our wives and children.

The American people sent the Long Hair [Lieutenant Colonel George Armstrong Custer] to follow us. Do you know of anything we did to bring the Long Hair upon us at the Little Bighorn River? No, you don't. We were assembled there in a peaceable camp, hunting for meat to feed our families. What stories did your people hear that they sent the Long Hair upon us? Who told you these stories? If you were ever told that we were hostile, [then] it is a lie. Whoever told you so is a liar. It was a hunting camp. We had attacked nothing but the buffalo. It is for that I dislike the Americans. It is for their conduct towards me.

No, I do not want war with them. I am tired of war. I am tired of blood. I went with my people into the White Mother's country [of British Queen Victoria] so as to get away from war. If I had wanted to fight, [then] I would have stayed in my own country. We have come to hunt the buffalo. The buffalo have come down here [to the creek], and we follow them. We want meat. Our women and children are hungry. There is nothing for us but the wild game. We have not come to injure the white man or his property. We were forced to come [in search of food].

We have been told so, but we have come. If the Long Knives will let us hunt in peace, [then] we will go back as soon as we have got meat. We don't want the white man's blood. We don't want his horses. We want something to eat, and we must go where it is.

We will avoid them if we can. If we cannot, we will fight. I moved into the White Mother's country to get away from the Long Knives. They have followed me. They are making a soldiers' house [or a military outpost] close to the Assiniboine gift-house. It is to cut us off from the buffalo. They want us to starve.

Listen, friends. Your people wanted my country. I have given [some of] it to them. I have not sold it to them. I have given it to them. Then [I] went off on the prairie to hunt. Your people followed me. They drove me away. I fled before them and left the country behind me. They came close to the [border] line and built their soldiers' house. The buffalo have left us. We have followed them. Will your people not let us hunt in peace? We mean them no harm. The white men are safe. We do not want to steal your horses.

A border battle brought renewed attention to Sitting Bull and nearly roiled relations between the United States and Canada. Given a continuing diplomatic standoff, Colonel Nelson A. Miles vowed to stop Lakota incursions across the boundary line. Commanding some 700 infantry, cavalry, and artillery as well as 143 Crow, Cheyenne, and Assiniboine auxiliaries, he advanced northward from the upper Missouri River. On July 17, 1879, the Battle of Milk River allowed the US Army officer to boast of winning a swift victory against an old nemesis. His field cannons drove the "hostile Sioux" back to the Canadian side of the 49th parallel, as he dispatched Crow scouts to intercept them near Beaver Creek. Sitting Bull killed Magpie, a mounted Crow, during a dramatic duel on horseback. Afterward, Sitting Bull memorialized the confrontation in two groups of collected drawings. They heralded the chief's importance in defeating a "brave Indian." While showing himself adorned in a traditional headdress, Sitting Bull avoided rendering a scene that featured him shooting or killing any US regulars. A trader in Canada, Gus M. Hedderich, taught him to sign his name in English, which began to replace a conventional buffalo symbol in the autobiographical pictography. Completed at Fort Randall later, the drawings were donated eventually to the Bureau of American Ethnology.[5]

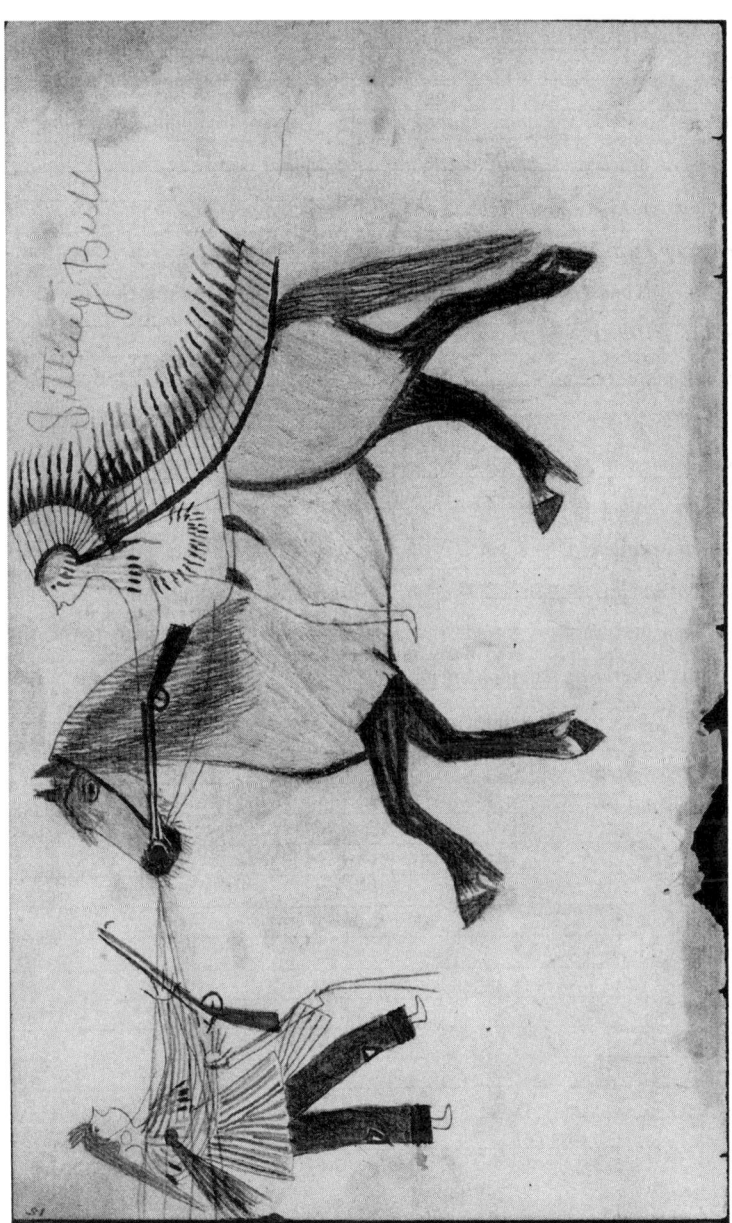

In battle with Crow scouts accompanying General Nelson A. Miles.

The free Lakota suffered from their Canadian asylum. Governmental officials wanted them to go back to the United States. The surge of refugees and stream of settlers near Wood Mountain strained resources. Overhunting diminished the bison, elk, moose, antelope, and fowl. Teetering on the brink of starvation, indigent families received limited assistance from nearby Métis and Francophone communities. Sitting Bull prayed while painting a buffalo robe, likely in 1880 or so. On a hide tanned by his wives, its imagery features a presumed self-portrait of the resilient chief with his Strong Heart bonnet. He sits below a feathered sun flanked by a sacred pipe on each side. Noble creatures such as a buffalo and an eagle appear on the margins. It is meant to be viewed from above, as onlookers gather in a circle. It was produced in consultation with the elders of a camp, possibly signaling the persistence of spiritual strength. It alludes to the performance of a sun dance, which marked an annual gathering to awaken the Earth. It is the only known buffalo hide painting by Sitting Bull that remains in existence. The cultural artifact, which Sitting Bull delivered to a trader in Canada, Gus M. Hedderich, entered the State Historical Society of North Dakota's collection in the twentieth century.[6]

Photograph of Buffalo Robe Painting by Sitting Bull.

Sitting Bull's camp had dwindled to no more than five hundred individuals by early 1881, when the Canadian government pressured them to leave the Wood Mountain area. At Willow Bunch, Jean Louis Legaré managed a trading post that provided food, water, and shelter for them temporarily. Running low on supplies, the trader suggested that they surrender to the US Army at Fort Buford. Sitting Bull left many of his followers at the trading post that spring, as he traveled northward to Qu'Appelle. His sixteen-year-old daughter, Many Horses, eloped with a warrior, joining a Legaré caravan that headed southward across the border. After returning to Willow Bunch that summer, Sitting Bull seemed devastated by the news of her departure. Several weeks of indecision elapsed, but he eventually joined another Legaré caravan on a border crossing. Major David H. Brotherton, the commanding officer at Fort Buford, dispatched a column with rations to meet them. On July 19, 1881, Sitting Bull and Legaré entered the military outpost while leading a procession of exactly 44 men, 143 women, and their children. The next day, a makeshift ceremony occurred in the officer's quarters. Crowded into a room, an interpreter and a newspaperman recorded what happened. Sitting Bull entered wearing a shabby blanket, calico shirt, and black pants. Major Brotherton invited him to speak.[7]

I surrender this rifle to you through my young son [Crow Foot], whom I desire to teach in this manner now that he has become a friend of the Americans. I wish him to learn the habits of the whites and to be educated as their sons are educated. I wish it to be remembered that I was the last man of my tribe to surrender my rifle. This boy has given it to you, and he now wants to know how he is going to make a living.

Whatever you have to give and whatever you have to say, I would like to receive or hear now, for I don't wish to be kept in darkness longer. I have sent several messengers in here from time to time, but none of them have returned with news. The other chiefs, Crow King and Gall, have not wanted me to come, and I have never received good news from here. I now wish to be allowed to live on this side of the [border] line, or the other, as I see fit. I wish to continue my old life of hunting but would like to be allowed to trade on both sides of the line.

This is my country, and I don't want to be compelled to give it up. My heart was very sad at having to leave the mother's country [of British Queen Victoria]. She has been a friend to me, but I want my children to grow up in my native country, and I wish also to feel that I can visit two of my friends on the other side of the line—Major [James M.] Walsh and Captain [Alexander] Macdonell—whenever I wish and would like to trade with [Jean] Louis Legaré, as he has always been a friend to me. I wish to have all my people live together upon one reservation of our own on the Little Missouri [River]. I left several families at Wood Mountain and between there and Qu'Appelle. I have many people among the Yanktonais at Poplar Creek, and I wish all of them and those who have gone to Standing Rock to be collected together upon one reservation. My people, many of them, have been bad [in the past]. All are good now that their arms and ponies have been taken from them.

You own this ground with me, and we must try and help each other. I do not wish to leave here until I get all the people I left behind. I would like to have my daughter, who is now at Fort Yates, sent up here to visit me, as also eight men; and I would like to know that Louis Legaré is to be rewarded for his services in bringing me and my people here.

At Fort Buford, Sitting Bull boarded a downriver steamer named the General Sherman. When it stopped at Bismarck in the Dakota Territory, the curious populace gathered along the waterfront to glimpse the subdued Lakota. Afflicted with a severe eye infection, he wore a pair of smoked goggles. He toured the frontier town, examined a railroad car, and dined at the Merchant's Hotel. He sold his autograph and other items to bystanders before returning to the steamer. After disembarking at Fort Yates, he encamped about a half-mile from the Missouri River. "It is all of one piece," he complained, since the Americans "have always lied to me." Sitting on a sandy river bank, he smoked a pipe while brooding. US soldiers kept a watch on him. He reunited with his daughter Many Horses, who left her husband and rejoined his household. He reminisced with Gall, Crow King, and Running Antelope. Charging a fee, he sat for portraits by Orlando S. Goff, a photographer. On August 2, 1881, Sitting Bull invited a Minnesota correspondent to conduct an interview inside his tipi. More than a dozen people observed it, including One Bull, Four Horns, and Bone Tomahawk. Edward "Fish" Allison, a longtime scout on the upper Missouri, interpreted the Siouxan language for the correspondent.[8]

I don't know where I was born and cannot remember. I know that I was born, though, or [I] would not be here. I was born of a woman. I know this is a fact, because I exist. (A side conversation with Four Horns ensued.)

I was born near old Fort George [or Fort Pierre] on Willow Creek, below the mouth of the Cheyenne River. I am forty-four years-old as near as I can tell; we count our years from the moons between great events. The event from which I date my birth is the year [1837 or so] in which Thunder Hawks was born. I am as old as he. I have always been running around. Indians that remain on the same hunting grounds all the time can remember the years better. I have nine children and two living wives and one wife that has gone to the Great Spirit. I have two pairs of twins. I think as much of them as the others. If I did not, I would not keep them. I think if I had a white wife, I would think more of her than the other two. Was-Seen-by-the-Nation is the name of the old one. The-One-That-Had-Four-Robes is the name of the other.

My father and two uncles were chiefs. My father's name was Jumping Bull. My uncle that is in the tipi [with me] is called Four Horns, and my other uncle was called Hunting His Lodge [or Looks-for-Him-in-a-Tent]. My father was a very rich man and owned a great many good ponies in four colors. In ponies he took much pride. They were roan, white, and gray. He had great numbers and never wanted for a horse to ride.

When I was ten years old, I was famous as a hunter. My specialty was [hunting] buffalo calves. I gave the calves I killed to the poor, who had no horses. I was considered a good man. My father died twenty-one years ago. For four years after I was ten years old, I killed buffalo and fed his people and thus became one of the fathers of the tribe. At the age of fourteen, I killed an enemy and began to make myself great in battle and became a chief. Before this, from [age] ten to fourteen, my people called me Sacred Standshot. After killing an enemy, they called me *Tatáŋka Íyotake*, or Sitting Bull. An Indian may be a hereditary chief, but he must make himself a chief by his bravery. (He was reluctant to speak of life beyond age fourteen.)

When I came in to [Fort] Buford, I gave up everything. I even gave up all my knives but this [one]. This is the only weapon I have. It is not sharp; I keep it to fix pipes. There were five great chiefs of the Sioux nation before me. They were *He-to* [meaning Four Horns], *Ce-su-ho-tan-ka* [meaning Loud Voiced Hawk], *Hclo-ta* [meaning Scarlet Horn], *Can-te-tanka* [meaning Big Heart], and *Ta-to-ka-en-yan-ka* [meaning Running Antelope]. All are dead but Running Antelope and Four Horns. He is the bravest chief beside myself. Antelope is *witko* [meaning a fool]. He has been among the whites and asked all of us to surrender.

Already have I told my reasons [for crossing the border]. I was not raised to be an enemy of the whites. These five chiefs that I have named were not enemies of the white man. The palefaces had things that we needed in order to hunt. We needed ammunition. Our interests were in peace. I never sold that much land (picking up a little dirt and letting it fall and blow away). I never made or sold a treaty with the United States. I came in [to Fort Buford] to claim my rights and the rights of my people. I was driven by force from my land, and I now come back to claim it for my people. I never made war on the United States government. I never stood in the white man's country. I never committed any depredations in the white man's country. I never made the white man's heart bleed. The white man came on to my land and followed me. The white men made me fight for my hunting grounds. The white man made me kill him, or he would kill my friends, my women, and my children. There was a Great Spirit, who guided and controlled that battle [along the Greasy Grass]. I could do nothing [without *Wakantanka*]. I was sustained by the Great Mysterious One. (He pointed upward with his forefinger.)

I was not a white man, for the Great Spirit did not make me a white skin. I did not fight [behind] the white man's back. I came out and met him on the grass. When I say Running Antelope is a fool, I mean he made treaties and allowed the white man to come in and occupy our land. Ever since that time, there has been trouble. I do not want aid or assistance from the whites or anyone else. I want them to stay [away] from my country and allow me to hunt on my own land. I want no blood spilled in my land except the blood of the buffalo. I want to hunt and trade for many moons. You have asked me to come in. I wanted the white man to provide for me for several years if I came in. You have never offered me any inducements to come in. I did not want to come. My friends that come got soap and ax handles but not enough [food] to eat. I have come in and want the white man to allow me to hunt in my own country. That is the way I live. I want to keep my ponies. I can't hunt without ponies. The buffalo runs fast. The white man wanted me to give up everything.

I expected to stay but a few days at [Fort] Buford. When I came in, I did not surrender. I want the government to let me occupy the Little Missouri country. There is plenty of game there. I have damages against the government for holding my land and game. I want the Great Father [or the US president] to pay me for it. My hunting ground is from the Badlands to the end of the Little Missouri [River], and I want it extended down here, where some of my people are, so that I can trade. Antelope is a fool. I have seen Gall. He can't tell me anything. He is not a chief of my people. I have not had a chance to talk with them [at Fort Yates]. They are waiting for me to speak. They want to give me a feast and hold a council. I am not jealous of them. I do not know whether we will hold a council or not.

I am not afraid to talk about that [battle along the Greasy Grass]. It all happened. It is passed and gone. I do not lie but do not want to talk about it. Low Dog says I can't fight until someone lends me a heart. Gall says my heart is no bigger than that (placing one forefinger at the base of the nail of another finger). We have all fought hard. We did not know [Lieutenant Colonel George Armstrong] Custer. When we saw him, we threw up our hands [in prayer]; and I cried, "Follow me, and do as I do." We whipped each other's horses, and it was all over. There was not as many Indians as the white man says. They are all warriors. There was not more than 2,000. Crow King speaks the truth; I did not want to kill any more men. I did not like that kind of work. I only defended my camp. When we had killed enough [in self-defense], that was all that was necessary. (He did not want to say any more about the battle.)

Yes, I have seen the great newspapers [while] over there [on the other side of the border]. I have never talked to a reporter [on this side] before. None of them ever before paid me money. My words are worth dollars.

If the Great Father gives me a reservation, [then] I do not want to be confined to any part of it. I want no restraint. I will keep on the reservation but want to go where I please. I don't want a white man over me. I don't want an agent. I want to have the white man with me but not to be my chief. I ask this, because I want to do right by my people and can't trust anyone else to trade with them or talk to them. I want interpreters to talk to the white man for me and [to] transact my business, but I want it to be seen and known that I have my rights. I want my people to have light wagons to work with. They do not know how to handle heavy wagons with cattle. We want light wagons and ponies. I don't want to give up game, as long as there is any game. I will be half-civilized till the game is gone. Then I will be all civilized. I want peace and no trouble. I want to raise my children, [so] that they may have peace and prosperity. I like the way the white brother keeps his children. Miss Fanny Culbertson of Poplar River was the first person I shook hands with when I came over the line.

My daughter [Many Horses] came to see me last night. We both cried. I was happy to see her. The [US] soldiers would not let her come into my camp at first. She came here before I did, and I listened a long time to hear words from her and for the winds to tell me how she was treated. I did not hear. I came down to see her. She seems to be doing well, but I saw she had no respect from the whites. The soldiers would not spread down a blanket for her to walk into my camp. She is well dressed, but she says her relatives at the agency gave her clothes.

[With regard to the shooting of US President James A. Garfield,] it was a cowardly act. If the warrior had been there, he would have gone to the Great Father's face and looked him in the eyes and then shot him. I heard when way up there [north] about the Great Father being shot but had no one to tell me all about it. I don't know whether the warrior was wise in doing it or not. He might have shot the Great Father, because he was not treating the Indians right. If that was so, it was not a bad thing to do. If a coward should shoot one of our chiefs or warriors without looking him in the eyes, our friends would go and kill him. If he was a very rich coward, he could pay the damages in many ponies, and we would let him leave.

I have killed sixteen enemies. I never killed a white man. I have made raids upon the Crees, Gros Ventres, and Northern Blackfeet and have stolen horses twenty-two times. I never stole horse from the whites.

I have told you all I want. I would like to have the Great Father listen to what I have said and help me accomplish what I ask.

Newspapers across the country reported that Sitting Bull remained belligerent and that his subordinates intended "mischief." Though no longer potent as a military threat, his "medicine power" remained in high regard among the Lakota. Angered by the imperious decrees of the US government, he announced that he would die like Crazy Horse if necessary. Near Fort Yates, a multitude of warriors grew restless and contemplated violence. Employed to conduct a census for administrative purposes, William T. Selwyn, "a full-blooded" Yankton Sioux with a formal education, agreed to meet personally with Sitting Bull. On August 26, 1881, the latter directed the former to transcribe a message to be sent to the Great Father in Washington DC. Indeed, he asked for a one-on-one meeting with the commander in chief. Even if translated into English accurately by Selwyn, the words made no difference to the War Department. The post commander, Colonel Charles C. Gilbert, refused to appease the angry chief. Two weeks later, the General Sherman *docked at Fort Yates to transport its reluctant passengers down the river to Fort Randall. A line of bluecoats fixed their bayonets, forcing Sitting Bull toward the gangway. US soldiers carried him across the plank. With 167 others herded on board, the steamer delivered the prisoners of war to a military stockade.*⁹

For the last few years I have been in the north, where there are plenty of buffalo, for the buffalo were my means of living. God [Wakantanka] made me to live on the flesh of the buffalo, so I thought I would stay there as long as there were buffalo enough for us. But the Great Father [or the US president] sent for me several times, and although I did not know why he wanted me to come down, I consented to do so.

I never, myself, made war against the children of the Great Father, and I never sought a fight with them. While I was looking for buffalo, they would attack and shoot at me, and of course I had to defend myself or else I should die. But all the blame is put on me [unfairly].

I have always thought that the Dakotas were all one body, and I wanted to make an agreement with them to come and settle down. While I have been in the north, here and there, a good many little things have happened, and I have been blamed for them; but I know that I am innocent. Those men who have made the trouble ought to be blamed. Everybody knows that I was not going to stay in the north any longer, but that when the buffalo disappeared I should make up my mind to come down [south of the border].

Although you [William T. Selwyn] are a Dakota, you are employed by the Great Father; therefore, I want you to let him hear my words. When I first came down, white men came to me almost every day to get some words out of me, but I said: "No. When I settle down, I shall say some words to the Great Father." I know that some white rascals have dealt with the Dakotas and by their foolish ways have ruined them. As for myself, I do not want anyone to do [anything] mischievously or deceitfully. So, I do not want to let any ordinary man hear my words. I tell the whites that my words are worth something; and even if they were willing to pay me for it, I never made any reply. But as soon as I saw you, I was well pleased. Although you are a Dakota, you have gathered up many good words and put them into my ears. Today, I was wishing that someone would come in and advise me; and as you have done so, it pleases me very much. All the people here belong to me, and I hope that the Great Father will treat them kindly. I always thought that when we came back and any of my relatives came to me with good words, I should reply, "Yes, yes." Today, you have put good words into my ears; and I have said, "Yes." In the future, I hope I shall have some good, honest, reliable men with me. Interpreters have come to me often, following me up [north]; and I have said, "No, I am not a child; if I want to do anything, I shall take time to think it over."

It is said that [Chief] Spotted Tail was killed [in 1881] by getting mixed up with bad men. Often times, a man has lost his life by being mixed up with bad men. But I wish that my people may be treated well so that they may do rightly. I am the last one that has come in from the north, and yet I wish to surpass the old agency Dakotas in what is right, and I wish that the Great Father would furnish me with farming implements so that I can till the ground.

My brother, I wish you would send this message to the Great Father right away so that he will help me. Now I have confidence in you that you will be able to send off my message. I am glad that you came to see me. It is a good thing for relatives to see each other. I have no objections to your numbering the people [for a census].

Situated on the west bank of the Missouri River, Fort Randall received the prisoners of war on September 17, 1881. They occupied thirty-two tipis close to the buildings, where they received daily rations but little else. The Twenty-Fifth Infantry, a unit of black soldiers, guarded their encampment. James Creelman, a correspondent for the New York Herald, visited the site a few weeks after Sitting Bull's arrival. His popular book of travel writing included a conversation with the Lakota leader, who allowed the stranger to enter his tipi to witness a ceremony. Several kinsmen sat in a circle with the solemn chief at the head. Seated nearby, Edward "Fish" Allison acted as an interpreter. Sitting Bull placed a tomahawk and knife on the ground before him. Staring into a small fire that had been kindled, he ruminated in silence. He began to fill a long pipe with tobacco, lit it, and puffed on it. He passed it to the others in the circle, as they smoked together without uttering a word. When he finally spoke in a deep, low voice, everybody nodded in agreement. According to Creelman, Sitting Bull knew "that nothing can compensate men for the loss of liberty and that everything else can be endured but that."[10]

I have lived a long time, and I have seen a great deal, and I have always had a reason for everything I have done. Every act of my life has had an object in view, and no man can say that I have neglected facts or failed to think.

I am one of the last chiefs of the independent Sioux nation, and the place I hold among my people was held by my ancestors before me. If I had no place in the world, [then] I would not be here, and the fact of my existence entitles me to exercise any influence I possess. I am satisfied that I was brought into this life for a purpose; otherwise, why am I here?

This land belongs to us, for the Great Spirit gave it to us when he put us here. We were free to come and go and to live in our own way. But white men, who belong to another land, have come upon us and are forcing us to live according to their ideas. That is an injustice; we have never dreamed of making white men live as we live.

White men like to dig in the ground for their food. My people prefer to hunt the buffalo, as their fathers did. White men like to stay in one place. My people want to move their tipis here and there to the different hunting grounds. The life of white men is slavery. They are prisoners in towns or farms. The life my people want is a life of freedom. I have seen nothing that a white man has—houses or railways or clothing or food—that is as good as the right to move in the open country and live in our own fashion.

Why has our blood been shed by your soldiers?

(Sitting Bull drew a square on the ground with his thumb nail. Onlookers craned their necks to see what he was doing.)

There! Your soldiers made a mark like that in our country and said that we must live there. They fed us well and sent their doctors to heal our sick. They said that we should live without having to work. But they told us that we must go only so far in this direction and only so far in that direction. They gave us meat, but they took away our liberty. The white men had many things that we wanted, but we could see that they did not have the one thing we liked best—freedom. I would rather live in a tipi and go without meat when game is scarce than give up my privileges as a free Indian, even though I could have all that white men have. We marched across the lines of our reservation, and the soldiers followed us [to the Greasy Grass]. They attacked our village, and we killed them all. What would you do if your home was attacked? You would stand up like a brave man and defend it. That is our story.

I have spoken.

> The prisoners of war at Fort Randall resided in an encircled camp, where sentries patrolled the perimeter of the tipis. Sitting Bull exited his abode each morning, lifted his arms toward the sun, and sang his prayer of thanksgiving to Wakantanka. A cavalcade of guests visited him from time to time, including a bespectacled German named Rudolf Cronau but called Ista-masa, or "Iron Eyes," by the Lakota. Sitting Bull invited Cronau for "a most pleasant talk" inside his tipi. The former agreed to sit for a portrait, which the latter began sketching on October 25, 1881. The finished lithograph revealed a regal figure wearing a feathered warbonnet and ermine-tail pendants. Discussion ensued about artistic techniques for depicting horses, which possibly influenced the chief's drawings thereafter. The two men endeavored to teach each other their respective languages, speaking in private if the official interpreter was away. One Siouxan phrase that they shared in casual conversations was "How cola," or "Hello friend." Sitting Bull may have entrusted Cronau as a courier to pass along a message to US President Chester A. Arthur. Cronau departed Fort Randall in mid-November and returned to Germany in 1883. Even if some of the written exchanges insinuate the stylings of a dime-novelist, Sitting Bull kept the foreigner's photograph as a memento.[11]

I never was afraid of my enemies and did my best. My successes I owe to the Great Spirit.

Iron Eyes, when you go to the Great Father [or the US president], I beg you speak in my interest, for I am of the opinion that up to now no one has brought my wishes before the Great Father. Tell him that he may allow me to visit to speak with him personally. Tell him that I should like to live like a white man and own a farm that could feed me [with crops and livestock], for I do not want to live on rations given to us daily. I like to help myself. I should like to live on the Cannonball [River] or Grand River. There is good land, water, and wood. There also is the place where I was born. I wished that teachers might live there, who would teach my children and those of my warriors; further, I should like that blacksmiths and traders would settle there with whom I could establish connections.

Tell the Great Father that I do not speak only to speak. My heart is just, and [I] want what I say.

> The US government insisted that Sitting Bull might pose a danger to non-Indians and continued to detain him at Fort Randall. The post commander, Colonel George L. Andrews, initially turned away a delegation of Yankton Sioux seeking to interact with the Lakota prisoners. Worried about their traditional attire, he would permit them to walk the grounds—in his exact words—only if "dressed as white men." Evidently, the delegation complied with the officer's request, for a meeting occurred at the military outpost. Walking Elk, a literate member of the delegation, was permitted to write down a speech given by Sitting Bull. Running Bull, another visiting Yankton, witnessed the translation and transcription of the Lakota's words. After December 3, 1881, the US Army officer forwarded copies up the chain of command. Thanks to the penmanship of others, Sitting Bull began petitioning officials in Washington DC to allow him to live peaceably in "the home of his people." Old Strike-the-Ree, chief of the Yankton Sioux living across the Missouri River, added to the flood of correspondence, asking in a letter to Secretary of War Robert T. Lincoln: "What has Sitting Bull been convicted of doing that you hold him a prisoner of war for so many long moons?"[12]

From the days of my ancestors, the Nation of the Seven Council Fires of Aborigines [Očhéthi Šakówiŋ], who understand each other's language, have been accustomed to trade with the white people and to be on good terms with them. And after I grew up, I was always dealing with the traders and on good terms with them.

Then there came the treaty-making men and the men with white man's ways, and many of my brethren sold their lands to the Grand Father [or the US president] and said they would settle down and be civilized. And they sent word to me to come down to them [on the reservation]. I said: Friends, wait a little. There are a great many buffalo up here yet. I want to eat meat a while yet. By and by, when you get fixed up and able to make a good living at civilized ways, I will come down to you, and then I will have my people learn how to make a living that way. So, I said and stayed out in the wilderness and hunted buffalo.

Then the soldiers came and hunted my tracks and as soon as they got in sight of me shot at me, and after they had done that my boys [or warriors] turned upon them. So, they chased me for a number of years. And now, they put all the blame of this thing upon me. But friends, I know very well that all the blame does not lie with me. The beginning of the evil was with some of my nation, who lived nearer the whites.

And so, I said I would leave that business and come down to where my friends were being civilized, and I sent that word all around and told my people to lay by their weapons, but they did not want to hear me. So, I said: Well, the Grand Father has been calling me to come for a good many years, let us go and see what he wants us for. For me, I will go down and get what he calls me for. And so, I sent word to my friends who were being civilized at Standing Rock, and Cheyenne River, and Pine Ridge, and Rosebud, and Lower Brule, and Crow Creek, and Yankton agency and told them to help me to [live a] civilized life.

So, I came down. And I saw a missionary, and he told me that the Grand Father had laid down the gun and that there would be no more hostility, and he said the Grand Father told him to tell me that and also to tell the Grand Father, and I told him in what country I wished to settle down to civilized ways. And so, I am thinking now how we can get settled down.

I want to settle down to farming with my nation [in the United States]. I know that it is only by the help of the Grand Father, and so I want him to help them that they may live. And so, I want the Grand Father to give them some of his things. I want him to give a span of horses to each family, and a yoke of oxen, and a couple of plows, and a cow to each. And I want him to give them such things as they will need to live on for a number of years. And I want the Grand Father to give us a location for ourselves, where we can have these things.

Then I want to be good friends with the whites—the same as all the treaty Indians. Then I want my people to dress up like white people and live like they do. If I did not want to, [then] I would not have come down.

Then I want to make all these arrangements for my people; and in order to do this, I want to go and see the Grand Father [in Washington DC]. I want to go soon this winter, so [that] my people will be ready to settle down and go to work in the spring. I have given up everything my nation had to the Grand Father, so I want to go and see him.

Then my friends, now I have settled down to be civilized, I want my children taught. I want schools and teachers the same [as] you have. That is what I understand the Grand Father wanted me to come in for. So, I want my children to have those advantages.

Then I did not come in with one tribe alone. There were some with me from all the agencies, Standing Rock, Cheyenne River, Red Cloud, Spotted Tail, Lower Brule, Crow Creek, and Yankton, and it is with them all that I want the Grand Father to make the same provisions.

That is all.

PART 4

STANDING ROCK

While enduring nineteen months in military custody at Fort Randall, Sitting Bull tried to deal with the adverse circumstances. In early 1883, he dictated the names of trustworthy headmen and subchiefs to Lieutenant Colonel Peter T. Swain, the new post commander. He expressed a willingness to work with the Office of Indian Affairs but only if returned respectfully to a reservation and acknowledged properly as the head chief. He wanted to draw supplies for regular distribution, freeing his people from the uncertainties of a government dole. Cultural survival would require adjustments, he realized. Scribbled across long-ruled notebook paper, the memorandum in the US Army officer's handwriting outlined "the urgent request of Sitting Bull." Thanks to an endorsement from Secretary of War Robert T. Lincoln, Secretary of the Interior Henry M. Teller finally transferred the prisoners of war to the supervision of civilian authorities. A military detail from the Fifteenth Infantry escorted them on board the steamboat W. J. Behan, which Captain Grant Marsh piloted. They arrived at Fort Yates on May 10, 1883, and camped alongside the headquarters of the Standing Rock agency. The next day, Sitting Bull entered the office of Agent James McLaughlin for an hour-long talk. A small contingent of Hunkpapa and an agency interpreter, Phillip Wells, attended.[1]

It is God's [Wakantanka's] will that I should be the chief of all my people. I want to live henceforth at peace with all men, and I desire that all the people belonging to me on this reservation—they are scattered now among many bands—be gathered together so that I may be their chief. It is necessary that this should be so. I cannot keep my young men from doing wrong unless they are where I can control them. If they do wrong, or I do, I want you to tell me about it, and if you do wrong I'll come and tell you. I love and pity my people, and I want you to do the same [for them].

When I was a prisoner at [Fort] Randall, I got a letter from the Great Father [or the US president] saying that I was to be freed and sent back here, and that I should have oxen, wagons, and farming implements given [to] me, and I would like to get those things as well as any others that may be due me from the agency stores. I want to wear the same kind of clothes that you do and to wash them, when soiled, until they wear out. I want to go to Washington [DC], see the Great Chief and have a talk with him. I was a prisoner when the commissioners [Newton Edmunds, Peter C. Shannon, and James Teller] treated [or negotiated] with my people for the lands to be taken from the reservation, but I wrote the Great Father and told him I didn't like the way they were acting. In the same letter, I told him my objections to the killing of game by the whites.

I am a great chief, and I want to be rich. Then I can keep my people straight. Still, I can't watch all my Indians any more than the Great Father can watch all his agents. I have here a paper given [to] me by Colonel [Peter T.] Swain at Fort Randall, on which he has written the names of those men whom I want to have made chiefs under me.

Dominating Indian affairs at Standing Rock, Agent James McLaughlin vowed to "break" Sitting Bull. His Dakota wife, Marie Louise Buisson, advised him on Lakota politics, especially with regard to its factionalism and rivalries. His disregard for the "Big Chief" appeared in official reports, which noted "a very important personage" toiling in the fields with a hoe. The agent's patronage cultivated a number of compliant protégés, who undermined Sitting Bull's authority and deferred to federal mandates. At the same time, US commissioners intended to persuade the Lakota to sign an agreement to open up more reservation lands to non-Indian settlement. The US Senate dispatched a select committee, which was chaired by Massachusetts Senator Henry L. Dawes. They held a formal meeting at Standing Rock on August 22, 1883, when Sitting Bull, once again, stood in defiance of governmental coaxing. As the courtly senators permitted the interpreters to translate his indignant oratory, the assembled body of Plains Indians departed the meeting with a wave of his hand. Illinois Senator John A. Logan, a Civil War veteran and a founder of the Grand Army of the Republic, scolded Sitting Bull in public, threatening to confine him in the guardhouse for insubordination. Even if the politicians insisted that Sitting Bull was "not a great chief," the Lakota refused to be silenced.[2]

Of course, I will speak to you if you desire me to do so. I suppose it is only such men as you desire to speak who must say anything. Do you know who I am, that you speak as you do? Do you recognize me; do you know who I am? You say you know I am Sitting Bull, but do you know what position I hold?

I am here by the will of the Great Spirit, and by his will I am a chief. My heart is red and sweet, and I know it is sweet, because whatever passes near me puts out its tongue to me; and yet you men have come here to talk with us, and you say you don't know who I am. I want to tell you that if the Great Spirit has chosen anyone to be chief of this country, it is myself. Yes, that is all right. You have conducted yourselves like men who have been drinking whiskey, and I came here to give you some advice.

(Sitting Bull waved his hand and at once the Indians left the room in a body. Later, Sitting Bull returned to the room.)

I came in with a glad heart to shake hands with you, my friends, for I feel bad that I have displeased you; and I am here to apologize to you for my bad conduct and to take back what I said. I will take it back, because I consider I have made your hearts bad. I heard that you were coming here from the Great Father's house [in Washington DC] some time before you came, and I have been sitting here like a prisoner waiting for someone to release me. I was looking for you everywhere, and I considered that when we talked with you it was the same as if we were talking with the Great Father [or the US president]; and I believe that what I pour out from my heart the Great Father will hear. What I take back is what I said to cause the people to leave the council and want to apologize for leaving myself. The people acted like children, and I am sorry for it. I was very sorry when I found out that your intentions were good and entirely different from what I supposed they were. Now I will tell you my mind, and I will tell everything straight. I know the Great Spirit is looking down upon me from above and will hear what I say. Therefore, I will do my best to talk straight; and I am in hopes that someone will listen to my wishes and help me to carry them out.

I have always been a chief and have been made chief of all the land. Thirty-two years ago, I was present at councils with the white man, and at the time of the Fort Rice council I was on the prairies listening to it, and since then a great many questions have been asked me about it, and I always said wait; and when the Black Hills council was held, and they asked me to give up that land, I said they must wait. I remember well all the promises that were made about that land, because I have thought a great deal about them since that time. Of course, I know that the Great Spirit provided me with animals for my food, but I did not stay out on the prairie, because I did not wish to accept the offers of the Great Father, for I sent in a great many of my people, and I told them that the Great Father was providing for them and keeping his agreements with them, and I was sending the Indians word all the time I was out that they must remember their agreements and fulfill them and carry them out straight. When the English authorities were looking for me, I heard that the Great Father's people were looking for me, too. I was not lost. I knew where I was going all the time.

Previous to that time, when a Catholic priest called "White Hair" [Bishop Martin Marty] came to see me, I told him all these things plainly. He told me the wishes of the Great Father, and I made promises which I meant to fulfill and did fulfill; and when I went over into the British possessions [in Canada] he followed me, and I told him everything that was in my heart and sent him back to tell the Great Father what I told him; and General [Alfred H.] Terry sent me word afterwards to come in, because he had big promises to make me, and I sent him word that I would not throw my country away; that I considered it all mine still, and I wanted him to wait just four years for me; that I had gone over there to attend to some business of my own, and my people were doing just as any other people would do.

If a man loses anything and goes back and looks carefully for it, he will find it, and that is what the Indians are doing now when they ask you to give them the things they were promised in the past. And I do not consider that they should be treated like beasts, and that is the reason I have grown up with the feelings that I have. Whatever you wanted of me I have obeyed, and I have come when you called me. The Great Father sent me word that whatever he had against me in the past had been forgiven and thrown aside, and he would have nothing against me in the future, and I accepted his promises and came in. And he told me not to step aside from the white man's path, and I told him I would not, and I am doing my best to travel in that path.

I feel that my country has gotten a bad name, and I want it to have a good name. It used to have a good name, and I sit sometimes and wonder who it is that has given it a bad name. You are the only people now who can give it a good name, and I want you to take care of my country and respect it. When we sold the Black Hills [in the Agreement of 1877], we got a very small price for it and not what we ought to have received. I used to think that the size of the payments would remain the same all the time, but they are growing smaller all the time. I want you to tell the Great Father everything I have said and that we want some benefits from the promises he has made to us. And I don't think I should be tormented with anything about giving up any part of my land until those promises are fulfilled. I would rather wait until that time, when I will be ready to transact any business he may desire.

I consider that my country takes in the Black Hills and runs from the Powder River to the Missouri [River] and that all of this land belongs to me. Our reservation is not as large as we want it to be, and I suppose the Great Father owes us money now for land he has taken in the past. You white men advise us to follow your ways, and therefore I talk as I do. When you have a piece of land and anything trespasses on it, you catch it and keep it until you get damages, and I am doing the same thing now. And I want you to tell this to the Great Father for me. I am looking into the future for the benefit of my children, and that is what I mean when I say I want my country taken care of for me. My children will grow up here, and I am looking ahead for their benefit and for the benefit of my children's children, too; and even beyond that again.

I sit here and look around me now, and I see my people starving, and I want the Great Father to make an increase in the amount of food that is allowed us now, so that they may be able to live. We want cattle to butcher—I want you to kill 300 head of cattle at a time. That is the way you live, and we want to live the same way. This is what I want you to tell the Great Father when you go back home. If we get the things we want, [then] our children will be raised like the white children. When the Great Father told me to live like his people, I told him to send me six teams of mules, because that is the way white people make a living, and I wanted my children to have these things to help them to make a living. I also told him to send me two spans of horses with wagons and everything else my children would need. I also asked for a horse and buggy for my children. I was advised to follow the ways of the white man, and that is why I asked for those things. I never asked for anything that is not needed. I also asked for a cow and a bull for each family, so that they can raise cattle of their own. I asked for four yokes of oxen and wagons with them. Also, [I asked for] a yoke of oxen and a wagon for each of my children to haul wood with. It is your own doing that I am here. You sent me here and advised me to live as you do, and it is not right for me to live in poverty. I asked the Great Father for hogs, male and female, and for male and female sheep for my children to raise from. I did not leave out anything in the way of animals that the white men have; I have asked for every one of them. I want you to tell the Great Father to send me some agricultural implements, so that I will not be obliged to work bare-handed. Whatever he sends to this agency, our agent will take care of for us, and we will be satisfied, because we know he will keep everything right. Whatever is sent here for us, he will be pleased to take care of for us.

I want to tell you that our rations have been reduced to almost nothing, and many of the people have starved to death. Now I beg of you to have the amount of rations increased, so that our children will not starve but will live better than they do now. I want clothing, too, and I will ask for that, too. We want all kinds of clothing for our people. Look at the men around here and see how poorly dressed they are. We want some clothing this month, and when it gets cold, we want more [blankets] to protect us from the weather. That is all I have to say....

I have just one more word to say. Of course, if a man is a chief and has authority, he should be proud and think himself a great man.

> *By the spring of 1884, Sitting Bull had decided to live about forty miles southwest of the Standing Rock agency headquarters. His brother-in-law Gray Eagle offered him a log cabin on the north bank of the Grand River. In addition to providing him a residence, the estate included horses, cattle, and chickens. His family cultivated productive fields of oats, corn, and potatoes. As time passed, he directed the building of a shed in addition to the digging of a cellar. Christian missionaries established churches and schools in the vicinity, as Catholics, Episcopalians, Presbyterians, and Congregationalists competed to win converts. Though reluctant to endorse off-reservation boarding schools, Sitting Bull spoke positively about the educational opportunities closer to home. The five children in his household went to a day school. Within his inner circle, Jumping Bull and One Bull sent their children as well. Father Jerome Hunt, an intrepid black-robed priest and the eventual author of* Bible History in the Sioux Indian Language *(1897), invited Sitting Bull to a "big feed" at a Catholic schoolhouse. He asked to share a message with the students. Even if embroidered or embellished, his translated "advice" was recorded by E. D. White. Typically, Siouxan speakers refer to the nurturing of children as* wakan icaga, *which means that "something sacred is growing."*[3]

My dear grandchildren:

All of your folks are my relatives, because I am a Sioux, and so are they. I was glad to hear that the Black Robe had given you this school where you can learn to read, write, and count the way white people do. You are also being taught a new religion. You are shown how the white men work and make things. You are living in a new path.

When I was your age, things were entirely different. I had no teachers but my parents and relatives. They are dead and gone now, and I am left alone. It will be the same with you. Your parents are aging and will die someday, leaving you alone. So, it is for you to make something of yourselves, and this can only be done while you are young.

In my early days, I was eager to learn and to do things, and therefore I learned quickly, and that made it easier for my teachers. Now I often pick up papers and books, which have all kinds of pictures and marks on them, but I cannot understand them as a white person does. They have a way of communicating by the use of written symbols and figures; but before they could do that, they had to have an understanding among themselves. You are learning that [way], and I was very much pleased to hear you reading.

In the future, your business dealings with the whites are going to be very hard, and it behooves you to learn well what you are taught here. But that is not all. We older people need you. In our dealings with the white men, we are just the same as blind men, because we do not understand them. We need you to help us understand what the white men are up to.

My grandchildren, be good. Try and make a mark for yourselves. Learn all you can.

With all my heart, I thank my Black Robe friends for their goodness and kindness towards me.

> *Sitting Bull welcomed the opportunity to travel, because he profited from the sale of autographs to importuning strangers. For example, the Standing Rock agency sent him to a Dakota Territory celebration in Bismarck, the new capital. He rode a railway coach for the first time. After appearing at the fore of a parade, he spoke briefly to an anxious crowd in his own language. On March 14, 1884, the Northern Pacific Railroad provided his entourage with passes to visit St. Paul, Minnesota. He stayed at the Merchants Hotel for a couple of weeks. His guides to the city showed him a school, a cathedral, a church, a theater, an armory, a post office, a fire station, and the state capitol. He visited a grocery wholesaler, where shelves filled with foodstuff caught his attention. He walked through factories that produced clothing, shoes, and cigars. His sojourn involved stops at Fort Snelling and Minneapolis, Minnesota. He observed the technology of communication at the* Pioneer Press *building, even testing out a telephone with his nephew, One Bull. A few scribes recorded his commentary about "civilization." Of course, all quotations passed through two filters: the hired interpreters and the biased reporters. What Sitting Bull may have said before the filtering has been lost in translation.*[4]

I like white people very much, and I want my children to be raised among them. I think the white people ought to be well pleased with their country, [living] with all its civilization and improvement. I think the houses of the whites are very grand, their machinery curious and cunning. My first impression of the iron horse was that it was so fast I wanted to get out of its way as quickly as possible.

I am naturally wild and love wild country. I do not understand white ways. With my children, it will be different. I love my own country best and prefer to live there.

Well, we live, but I don't think that we get enough rations. I wonder why the Great Father [or the US president] does not give us more food. Our food is not enough; and if the Great Father does not give us more, we are likely to starve.

I wish to say that in our own country our white brothers killed the Sioux's buffaloes. Our young men took some buffalo skins, and the white men made us pay for them. I think the Great Father should command that we receive our money back and our loss on the account of the killing of the buffalo made good. I think he should order that no more buffaloes or game should be killed in our country by the white men.

I have come to tell One Star [Brigadier General Alfred H. Terry] how I and my people are getting along at the agency, so that he may go and repeat my words to the Great Father. I have been here but a short time, but I like it very much. The people are just as good here as they are in the other city.

> The Minnesota proprietor of the Merchants Hotel, Alvaren Allen, organized a moneymaking showcase called the "Sitting Bull Combination" in 1884. The tour began in St. Paul but swiftly proceeded eastward on the "iron horse." Gray Eagle, Flying By, Long Dog, Crow Eagle, and their wives made the railway trip. Moving from busy depots to packed theaters, Sitting Bull braided his hair with mink and otter and donned leggings, plaited with weasel skins and porcupine quills. After the train reached New York City that fall, he and his fellow travelers appeared before a capacity crowd at a wax museum. The promoters claimed that the proceeds from the gate supported Indian housing and agriculture around Standing Rock. The staging included a tipi in addition to fully dressed Indians, who cooked meals and smoked pipes in front of an enthralled audience. A hired interpreter delivered pre-written remarks that rarely resembled what the Lakota said. Luther Standing Bear, a young Oglala student at Carlisle Indian Industrial School, paid fifty cents to see Sitting Bull at the Association Hall in Philadelphia, Pennsylvania. While listening to the famous chief orate that September, he noted Siouxan phrases that reiterated a message of peace. The errant parsing by the given interpretations repeated so many lies, he mused, that "I had to smile."[5]

My friends, white people, we Indians are on our way to Washington [DC] to see the Grandfather, or President of the United States. I see so many white people and what they are doing that it makes me glad to know that someday my children will be educated also. There is no use fighting any longer. The buffalo are all gone—as well as the rest of the game.

Now I am going to shake the hand of the Great Father at Washington [DC], and I am going to tell him all these things.

William F. Cody managed a popular show called Buffalo Bill's Wild West, which hired Sitting Bull for its 1885 season. According to the contract, Sitting Bull earned $50 a week, a bonus of $125, and exclusive rights to the sale of his portraits and autographs. Touring more than a dozen cities in the United States and Canada, he mounted a steed for the opening act, greeted visitors at a tipi, and answered questions from the press. Eager to receive tribute from the Gilded Age spectators, he attempted to avoid controversies with his public statements. He demanded the hiring of William Halsey, an agency interpreter from Standing Rock, to assist him with personal communication. He referred to Cody as "Long Hair" in front of the reporters—the same label used for the slain cavalryman at the Little Bighorn River. In fact, the show manager admitted to a gaggle that "white men were responsible for the Sitting Bull War." Sitting Bull unofficially adopted performer Annie Oakley as a daughter, giving her the nickname "Little Sure Shot." The billed appearances generated excitement for the "equestrian extravaganza," but he grew homesick. Chafing from the irritations of show business, he was subjected to patronizing attitudes and annoying jeers. Buffalo Bill returned him to Standing Rock once the season ended, gifting him a white hat and a gray horse.[6]

I am fifty years of age. My father's name was Jumping Bull, and he was chief of the Sioux. When fourteen years of age, I went on my first warpath against a neighboring tribe. I distinguished myself for my bravery. My father upon my return called me before the tribe and gave me the name Sitting Bull. He gave away four horses to poor braves when he christened me. My father's name means a very strong man; my own signified that I am a powerful rider. My father died twenty-three years ago, and I became chief of my tribe. My mother died last year in her seventieth year. I have 5,000 people in my tribe [among the Lakota Sioux] with headquarters at Standing Rock agency, Dakota [Territory].

[The people of the United States are] as numerous as the flies that follow the buffalo. The Indians cannot fight them. The palefaces want the earth, the corn, the tree, the sky. Indians only want wide prairie, where he can live in peace and safety, where he shall not be disturbed, and where he can die. Indians only want justice. Palefaces feel kind [now] and will do us right.

Tanka, the Great Father [or the US president], is good. He orders cattle off our lands and protects us. Cattlemen steal our horses and cattle and kill our game and leave us to starve and die or fight. They rented land to two treacherous chiefs, who had no right to do it. The Great Father is good, and we will remember him.

[I want] to learn the way of the whites and teach my people how to live better. I go back in four weeks and [will] tell my people what I have seen. They will not go on the warpath again. I have learned much. Indians must keep quiet or die. The Great Father must protect us and give us justice.

Palefaces found gold on my land in the Black Hills. They drove us away, as they would dogs. They killed my people and stole our horses. I fought for my people. My people said I was right. I will always answer to my people. The friend of the dead palefaces must answer for those who are dead.

Yes, we were in camp with our squaws and children. [Lieutenant Colonel George Armstrong] Custer came over the divide and saw us. He charged. We surrounded him. He was killed with all his men. He intended [on] killing us. We had 4,000 warriors and 6,000 or 7,000 women and children in the camp. I had 600 warriors, and [I heard that] 207 died with Custer. The camp was four or five miles long, all in the valley of the Little Bighorn. We did what any race would have done. Custer intended to kill us and our children. He had only a handful of men. He was rash. He could not see his nose.

Nobody knows [who killed Custer]. Everybody fired at him. He was a brave warrior, but he made a mistake. No one could tell who hit him. The young men and squaws honored him as a great warrior. They did not scalp him. I don't like talking of that. . . .

I like the show business very well. But most every day now I think of my wives and children, and I want to see them. I had a daughter born three weeks ago. I think I will go back to my home at Standing Rock agency, Dakota [Territory], after the engagement in St. Louis, [Missouri,] is over.

I was in Washington [DC] last July. I liked the big white chief very well. I am pleased with all the people. I have been in Canada and the [United] States. The ladies and children shook hands with me and made me glad.

The white people are so many; if every Indian in the West killed one every step they took, the dead would not be missed among you. There are so many. When I came away [from Indian country], I didn't want my children to go to school. But now I want them to be educated like the white children are. I have eleven children and two wives. That is all I want to say.

On June 22, 1885, Buffalo Bill's Wild West reached Washington DC. For three days, Sitting Bull and the troupe visited the national capital. If given an opportunity, he intended to communicate the concerns of the Lakota to the federal government. While visiting the War Department, he met General Philip H. Sheridan, the commander of the US Army. He examined the Declaration of Independence in the State Department library, perhaps thinking about its historic articulation of freedom. His handlers promised to arrange an audience with the president of the United States, Grover Cleveland. He brought to the White House a signed letter, which had been crafted in "the Indian language" with the assistance of Nate Salsbury. It was penned on the stationery of "Buffalo Bill's Wild West, America's National Entertainment." Later, the Interior Department received the document but discounted its supplications. Returning to Standing Rock, Sitting Bull insisted that the Great Father recognized him as the greatest Indian alive. "He is inflated with the public attention he received," complained Agent James McLaughlin, threatening to confine the celebrated "head chief of all the Sioux" to the guardhouse. When William F. Cody attempted to hire Sitting Bull for the show again, civilian authorities concluded that "it would be unwise" to permit him to tour for another season.[7]

To my Great Father [or the US president]:

I know the Great Father is a great chief and has great power over every person in the whole country. I am very glad to see the Great Father and to shake hands with him.

I want to travel in all the large places, so that I can tell my people how the white people work and live. I want my people to get more rations, for as yet we cannot support ourselves but are trying hard to farm. My people ask me to ask the Great Father for this. The agent has tried to get all he can for us, but there are so many he cannot get everything. I want to ask for more farming machinery for myself. I also want to have the privilege of trading at any store near to my reservation. For trading at one store, they charge me whatever they want to, and I have to pay to[o] dear. I want to trade at the fort store and ask the Great Father to open it to my people, for he [as the quartermaster] is a much better man than we have on the reservation.

Our agent is good to me and my people. Our boundary lines only are half as far as I thought they would [be], reaching only on Cedar Creek and Cannonball [River] instead of the Little Missouri [River]. Will the Great Father please tend to this [boundary]?

We want to know where the money is for the Fort Pierre road through the country.

Yours respectfully,
Sitting Bull

Not wanting to speak ill of the government, Sitting Bull asserted the importance of peace and goodwill at Standing Rock. Wary of the "white man's road," he urged the practice of traditional dances—including the sun dance—as a matter of religious liberty. He requested an increase in ration and blanket distributions while giving away his money out of compassion. His physical health deteriorated, as he sometimes complained of chest pains and lung trouble. In spite of maladies, he visited Gros Ventre, Mandan, and Arikara Indians at Fort Berthold and eventually joined a Sioux delegation to the Crow Reservation in Montana Territory. The intertribal gatherings encouraged cooperation among former rivals, which surprised the Indian Office of the Interior Department. Even though Agent James McLaughlin endorsed Gall and John Grass as the titular chiefs at Standing Rock, Sitting Bull remained influential through the secretive group known as the Silent Eaters. In 1886, he met often with close allies such as Strike Kettle, Pass Beyond, Hungry Crow, Catches-the-Bear, and Black Bird. Sitting Bull's nephew White Bull resided with the Miniconjou band at the Cheyenne River agency yet stayed in touch through his uncle's network. Sharing oral testimony with writer Walter S. Campbell years later, he insisted that Sitting Bull found ingenious ways "to speak his mind."[8]

Ever since I have returned to my people, the Hunkpapa, I realized the most nonsensical manner in which our relatives are striving to stand in with the Indian agent. I may be foolish, but being an Indian—a Hunkpapa and not a foreigner—I believe in upholding the rights of the Indian.

When I was a boy, we used to play a game called *cankukomnipi*—keeping the top in motion. We had tops made out of buffalo horns, some from wood, and some from pipe stone. In spinning the top, we held the top between the fingers and turned it quickly to the right. Then as soon as it is in motion, we used a whip, a small graceful stick about two feet long with a strip or strips of buckskin tied at the end for a lash.

Every Indian boy knows how to spin a top. We would clear the snow away from the base ground, leaving enough snow in which we could spin our tops, and we would try to see who could spin and drive his top in motion the farthest. But the best contest was [when] we would clear a place on the ice or on the snow-covered ground, which we made smooth.

We would then break off some willow brushes and placed these in a circle like a corral. The inside of the circle was cleared away with nothing but ice on the surface. The inside circle was about four or five feet in diameter. We left an opening on one side about a foot wide. This was the entrance for the driving [of] the spinning top. Two or more can play this game. The party or the side [that] first succeeded driving the spinning top inside of the circle was the winner. Consequently, we did everything with our tops to obstruct the spinning top from entering the circle. The tops are supposed to be in motion all the time. If one stops—failing to keep up—he is disqualified. It was a game, where we made our tops knock each other to keep each other's top from entering.

This is the way our Indians are doing since they came on the reservation. The Indian agent's office is the circle [at Standing Rock]. They all want to get inside and become a favorite. But no sooner one does this, then they all knock on him and, consequently, a lot of them failed to enter. Some, who are more clever and sagacious, succeed [in] getting by [with] almost everything and become the Indian agent's favorite.

I stand no show of getting inside the circle. But so long as I know I am not betraying my people, I am satisfied to stay outside.

The US Congress passed the Dawes Act in 1887, when its sponsor, Senator Henry L. Dawes of Massachusetts, promised a final solution to the "Indian problem." Humanitarian reformers, commercial farmers, cattle ranchers, and railroad boosters lobbied the Indian Office of the Interior Department to dismember the Great Sioux Reservation. After carving out smaller enclaves for Standing Rock, Cheyenne River, Pine Ridge, Rosebud, Crow Creek, and Lower Brule, policymakers would place all "surplus" acres in the national domain for non-Indians to claim. The Sioux Agreement stipulated that the general allotment scheme required approval from at least three-fourths of the adult males. Seeking the statutory number of signatures, a US commission headed by Captain Richard Henry Pratt arrived at Standing Rock during the summer of 1888. Most of the chieftains refused to sign. However, Sitting Bull agreed to join a delegation of selected leaders on a trip to Washington DC. The Washington Post *provided coverage of the "private councils" that October, noting that he offered extensive opening remarks in his own language. Avoiding the risk of misrepresentation, he addressed federal officials in the Interior Department briefly. He shook hands with the secretary of the interior, William F. Vilas, but took a seat behind the "premier" mouthpieces of the Sioux delegation.*⁹

My friends:

I do not wish to make a long speech. I have but few words to say. I call you my friends, because I am one of your people. I belong to the Government of the United States. As we have our own views of this new law [called the Sioux Agreement], we wish to speak to you as man to man. I hope everything will be done in a quiet manner.

This is all I have to say.

Figureheads held titles among the Siouxan speakers and gained favors from the high-handed bureaucrats, even if Sitting Bull expected to remain a prominent chief among his people. While visiting Washington DC during the fall of 1888, he appreciated that the Lakota must take what they could get on the "white man's road." He likely hoped to delay a deal, intending to disrupt the staged signings back at Standing Rock. Though conciliatory at times, he did not bow to the pressure campaign. The Sioux delegation offered a counterproposal to seek immediate compensation from the United States, demanding an amount that exceeded $13 million in cash. A man behind a camera captured a group portrait, as the cohort posed on the steps of the Interior Department building. Appearing on the left side of the photograph, Sitting Bull stood somewhat apart. He donned a dark suit but wore a pair of beaded moccasins. His right hand held a hat, which blurred somewhat. The body language suggests his suspicions. Whereas his attitude in prior shots may have been contrived in studios, the optics from the national capital signaled a standstill. He joined the others on a choreographed stroll to the White House, where he proceeded to shake hands with governmental dignitaries. The visit concluded without a final agreement.[10]

Detail of the US commissioners and delegations of Sioux chiefs visiting Washington DC, October 13, 1888. Sitting Bull is standing far most left of the group (#27).

US commissioners and delegations of Sioux chiefs visiting Washington DC, October 13, 1888.

Both North Dakota and South Dakota readied for statehood in 1889, when the federal government refined elements of the Sioux Agreement. Even though countless Lakota opposed any formula to reduce their landholdings, Major General George Crook, commanding the Military Division of the Missouri, headed a US commission that met with leaders at the six agencies. The US Army officer known as "Three Stars" convened great feasts, lifted the bans on ceremonial dancing, and parleyed with wobbly headmen; but the proceedings ignored Sitting Bull on the Grand River. He sent trusted "school boys" to the daytime councils at Standing Rock, asking them to observe the talks and to take notes. In the evenings, John Lone Man, a Hunkpapa, heard Sitting Bull's protests to the Silent Eaters. Agent James McLaughlin staged a public signing at an agency warehouse on August 3, when Sitting Bull mounted a horse and rode into the line. The mob "stampeded," yet the police force, commanded by Lieutenant Bull Head, expelled the "troublemakers" immediately. While General Crook considered sending troops after Sitting Bull, commissioners thwarted the opposition without further unrest. The final tally revealed 4,463 signatures out of the 5,678 eligible to vote, more than enough for acceptance. "Three Stars" celebrated but died of heart failure the next year.[11]

Friends and Relatives:

Our minds are again disturbed by the Great Father's representatives [from the Crook Commission], the Indian agent, the squaw-men, the mixed-bloods, the interpreters, and the favorite ration-chiefs. What is it they want of us this time? They want us to give up another chunk of our tribal land. This is not the first time nor the last time. They will try to gain possession of the last piece of ground we possess. They are again telling us what they intend to do if we agree to their wishes. Have we ever set a price on our land and received such a value? No, we never did.

What we got under the former treaties were promises of all sorts. They promised how we are going to live peaceably on the land we still own and how they are going to show us the new ways of living—even told us how we can go to Heaven when we die. But all that we realized out of the agreements with the Great Father [or the US president] was [that] we are dying off in expectation of getting things promised us.

One thing I wish to state at this time is [that] something tells me that the Great Father's representatives have again brought with them a well-worded paper, containing just what they want but ignoring our wishes in the matter. It is this that they are attempting to drive us to [accept]. Our people are blindly deceived. Some are in favor of the proposition, but we who realize that our children and grandchildren may have a little longer [to live] must necessarily look ahead and flatly reject the proposition. I, for one, am bitterly opposed to it. The Great Father has proven himself an *Iktomi* [or a trickster] in our past dealings.

When the white people invaded our Black Hills country, our treaty agreements [from Fort Laramie] were still in force. But the Great Father has ignored it—pretending to keep out the intruders through military force, and at last failing to keep them out, they had to let them come in and take possession of our best part of our tribal possession. Yet, the Great Father maintains a very large standing army that can stop anything.

Therefore, I do not wish to consider any proposition to cede any portion of our tribal holdings to the Great Father. If I agree to dispose of any part of our land to the white people, [then] I would feel guilty of taking food away from our children's mouths, and I do not wish to be that mean. There are things they tell us [that] sound good to hear, but when they have accomplished their purpose, they will go home and will not try to fulfill our agreements with them.

My friends and relatives, let us stand as one family, as we did before the white people led us astray.

The Lakota were frustrated by the broken promises of the Crook Commission, as reports of Indian "outbreaks" circulated from agency to agency. Following a solar eclipse in Nevada, Wovoka, a Paiute holy man, spoke of his dream for pan-Indian salvation. Once the non-Indians vanished in an imminent apocalyptic event, he prophesied, a supernatural renewal of Heaven and Earth would reunite the living Indians with the dead. A Miniconjou Sioux named Kicking Bear traveled westward with a small party to meet the acclaimed prophet. Sitting Bull invited Kicking Bear, a trusted relative, to visit Standing Rock with the "good news," and he arrived at the Grand River camp on October 9, 1890. As he taught the wanagi wachipi ki, *or the "spirit dance," he described a special shirt that would protect them from harm. Whether or not Sitting Bull actually believed the "Messiah Craze," word reached the agency headquarters that he plotted "mischief." Accompanied by an interpreter, Louis Primeau, Agent James McLaughlin met with Sitting Bull at a dance circle on November 18, 1890. Their conversation lasted about an hour, when the latter made an offer that the former refused. It was memorialized in a report to Commissioner of Indian Affairs Thomas Jefferson Morgan the next day. Two decades later, McLaughlin referenced it in his memoir,* My Friend the Indian.[12]

I will make you a proposition, which will settle this question.

You go with me to the agencies to the west [of Standing Rock], and let me seek for the men who saw the Messiah. And when we find them, I will demand that they show him to us. And if they cannot do so, I will return and tell my people it is a lie. All practices of the Ghost societies would cease. But if found to be as professed by the Indians, they be permitted to continue their medicine practices and organize [dances] as they are now endeavoring to do. . . .

My heart inclines to do what you request [to come first to the agency headquarters], but I must consult my people. I would be willing to go with you now, but I cannot leave without the consent of my people. I will talk to the men [from the Silent Eaters] tonight, and if they think it advisable, I will go to the agency next Saturday.

Civilian authorities at Standing Rock kept Sitting Bull under surveillance, while thousands of bluecoats were deployed to patrol the reservations. On December 10, 1890, Major General Nelson A. Miles, commanding the Military Division of the Missouri, directed troops at Fort Yates to "secure" Sitting Bull. Colonel William F. Drum, the Fort Yates commander, readied a detachment for action, as Sitting Bull consulted with Bull Ghost, Black Bird, Spotted-Horn-Bull, and the Silent Eaters. The next day, Sitting Bull dictated a letter to his son-in-law Andrew Fox, who had been married to his recently deceased daughter, Walks Looking. Equipped with only limited English fluency, Fox struggled to write down the exact wording for his father in-law. Agent James McLaughlin received Sitting Bull's letter but rejected his request to visit the Pine Ridge agency. On December 15, 1890, the Lakota police entered Sitting Bull's cabin at the Grand River. Shortly before dawn, the heavily armed lawmen roused his household and forced him to the doorway. A crowd formed outside, voicing protests and carrying weapons. Shots rang out. A close-range firefight ensued, taking the lives of Sitting Bull and thirteen others. Family and friends of the murdered chief fled for their safety. After monitoring the situation from afar, US soldiers arrived at the crime scene.[13]

Dear sir:

I want to write to [you with a] few lines today and let you know something. I [am] meeting with all my Indians today and writing to you this order.

God [*Wakantanka*] made you all the white race and also made the red race and gave them both might and heart to know everything in the world. But whites [think they are] higher than the Indians. But today our father is helping us the Indians. So, we all the Indians know.

So, I think this way. I wish no one to come to [me] in my prayers with their guns or knives. So, all the Indians pray to God for life and try to find out [the] good road and do nothing wrong in their lives. This is what we want—to pray to God.

But you did not believe us. So, you must not say anything against our prayers, because we did not say anything against your prayers. You pray to

God. So [also] do all of the Indians. We both pray to only one God to make us [good].

Yet you, my friend today, you think I am a fool. You take some wise men among my people on your side, and you let the white people back East know. So, I know that. But I think that is all right, because [you think] I am foolish to pray to God.

So, you don't like me, my friend. So, I don't like [it] myself when someone is foolish. So, you are the same. You don't like me, because [you think] I am foolish. If I was not here, then the Indians would be civilized. But because I am here, all the Indians [are called] foolish.

I know this is all you put down in the newspapers back East. So, I see the papers, but I think it is all right. When you were here in my camp, you gave me good words about my prayers. And today you take it all back from me.

Also, I will let you know something. I have got to go to Pine Ridge agency and to know their prayers. So, I [have] let you know that. The policemen told me you [are] going to take all our ponies and guns, too. So, I want you [to] let me know about that.

I want [your] answer back soon.

Sitting Bull

POSTSCRIPT

SOMETHING SAID IN PASSING

Postscript • Something Said in Passing

Reverend William Henry Harrison Murray eulogized Sitting Bull for the New York World on December 21, 1890. Known as "Adirondack Murray" for his advocacy of the outdoor movement, he felt compelled to deliver a written message for the "George Washington of the Sioux nation." Revealing a rhetorical flourish, the Gilded Age perspective of the polymath conveyed a number of Anglophonic biases. Nevertheless, he wanted the readers to learn about the "medicine man" and the "plot to kill him." In the years before a murder most foul, "Adirondack Murray" and Sitting Bull posed together for photographs and sat down briefly for conversations. Although their different languages and religious traditions made their words fleeting, the good reverend observed that the "seer" held an office above all earthly ones. He denounced the "land grabbers," who coveted almost every acre of Indian country in the United States. The "lying, thieving Indian agents," he lamented, conspired to silence a prophet among his own people and manipulated the "renegades" of the Indian police. The public opinion of the frontier, which he blamed on "ignorance, credulity, and selfish greed," excused many crimes on the reservations born of "Satan and sin." By suffering from grave injustices, Sitting Bull had achieved a status comparable to other martyrs in history.[1]

I knew this man—knew him in relation to his high office among his people and in his elements as a man. As to his office or rank, I honored him. He filled a station older than human records. As a man, I admired him. . . .

Hence, by virtue of his office old as custom and tradition, this man, Sitting Bull, was counselor of chiefs, the Warwick [of English history] behind the throne stronger than the throne, the oracle of mysteries and of knowledge hidden from the mass, hidden even from chiefs, to whose words of advice and authority all listened as to the last and highest expression of wisdom.

Such was Sitting Bull as to his office, as interpreted and understood from a standpoint of knowledge of the religion, the traditions and the superstition of his people. That he was faithful to his high office all knew. He was in fact counselor of chiefs. That as Joshua did to Moses, so he in hour of battle. [The Old Testament leaders] upheld their arms till the sun went down, and the battle was lost or won. Let all who fought his tribe declare that the gods of his race found in him a high priest faithful to his trust none may ever deny. He lived, and he has died, a red man true to his office and his race. That leaf of laurel none can deny to his fame—not even his renegade murderers.

But no office, however great, is as great as the man if he fills it greatly, and this man, Sitting Bull, was greater as a man than he was even as a prophet. I met him often; I studied him closely....

In face, he was the only man I ever saw who resembled [William] Gladstone—large featured, thoughtfully grave, reflective, reposeful when unexcited. In wrath, his countenance was a collection of unexploded or exploding thunder—the awful embodiment of measureless passion and power. In conversation, he was deliberate, the user of few words but suave and low-voiced. In moments of social relaxation, he was companionable, receptive of humor, a genial host, [and] a pleasant guest. In his family, gentle, affectionate, and not opposed to merriment. When sitting in council, his deportment was a model; grave, deliberate, courteous to opponents, patient and kindly to men of lesser mind. I suggest that our Senators copy after him. In pride, he was equal to his rank and race, a rank to him level with a [Roman Catholic] pope and a race the oldest and bravest in the world. Of vanity, I never saw one trace in him. I would couple the word with [William] Gladstone or [Daniel] Webster as quickly as with him. He was never over-dressed. He wore the insignia of his office as a king his robes or a judge his gown. In eating, he was temperate; from spirituous drinks, an abstainer. His word once given was a true bond. He was a born diplomat. No foe ever fathomed his thought. I have watched him by the hour when I knew his heart was hot with wrath, but neither from eye nor lip nor cheek nor nostril nor sinewy hand might one get hint of the storm raging within. There was no surface to him. He was the embodiment of depths....

Here are some words of his. You can compare them with your orators' best:

> You tell me of the Mohawks. My [ancestral] fathers knew them. They demanded tribute of them. The Sioux laughed. They went to meet them: ten thousand horsemen. The Mohawks saw them coming, made them a feast, and returned home.

You tell me of the Abenakis. They are our [all?] the forefathers of all red men. They were the men \fathers and came from the East. They were born in the morni\wn. They The traditions of my people are full of the Abenakis. The world. cradles of our race.

And again:

What treaty that the whites have kept has the red man broken? N\ one.
What treaty that the whites ever made with us red men have they kept? Not one.
When I was a boy the Sioux owned the world. The sun rose and the sun set in their lands. They sent ten thousand horsemen to battle.
Where are the warriors today? Who slew them? Where are our lands? Who owns them? What white man can say I ever stole his lands or a penny of his money? Yet they say I am a thief. What white woman, however lonely, was ever when a captive insulted [or assaulted] by me? Yet they say that I am a bad Indian.
What white man has ever seen me drunk? Who has ever come to me hungry and gone unfed? Who has ever seen me beat my wives or abuse my children? What law have I broken?
Is it wrong for me to love my own? Is it wicked in me because my skin is red; because I am a Sioux; because I was born where my fathers lived; because I would die for my people and my country?

And again:

They tell you I murdered [Lieutenant Colonel George Armstrong] Custer. It is a lie. I am not a war chief. I was not in the battle that day. His eyes were blinded that he could not see. He was a fool, and he rode to his death. He made the fight, not I. Whoever tells you I killed the Yellow Hair is a liar.

But why tell more of this man? Does this generation love justice enough to ask that it be shown to the red men? Have we not as a people fixed the brutal maxim in our language: "That the only good Indian is a dead Indian?" We laugh at the saying now as a good jest, but the cheeks of our redden with shame when they read the coarse brutality of our own—the great Sioux was dead, that he was set upon in the midst of his family with his wives and children and relatives around him, that he had committed no overt act of war, that he was simply—so far as aught is known—moving himself [with] his kith and kin from the midst of cold, hunger, and peril, and that while doing this, a company of Indians—yclept Indian police—many of them despised renegades from his own tribe and enemies of his under cover of the United States flag and backed by a company of United States cavalry—placed suspiciously handy to see that the renegades from his tribe should not fail in killing him—they went to kill—had killed him, and I said—understanding the conditions and circumstances better than some—I said: "That is murder." And then I read in a great journal that "everybody is well satisfied with his death." And I cried out against the saying, as I had against the deed.

I read that they have buried his body like a dog's—without funeral rites, without tribal wail, with no solemn song or act. That is the deed of today. That is the best that this generation has to give to this noble historic character, this man who in his person ends the line of aboriginal sanctities older than the religion of Christian or Jew.

Very well. So, let it stand for the present. But there is a generation coming that shall reverse this judgment of ours. Our children shall build monuments to those whom we stoned, and the great aboriginals whom we killed will be counted by the future American as among the historic characters of the continent.

ENDNOTES

Introduction: A Lakota Life

1. This biographical summary of Sitting Bull draws largely from Ernie LaPointe, *Sitting Bull: His Life and Legacy* (Layton, UT: Gibbs Smith, 2009); Gary C. Anderson, *Sitting Bull and the Paradox of Lakota Nationhood*, 3rd ed. (New York: Pearson Longman, 2007); Robert M. Utley, *The Lance and the Shield: The Life and Times of Sitting Bull* (New York: Henry Holt, 1993); Stanley Vestal, *Sitting Bull: Champion of the Sioux*, 2nd ed. (Norman: University of Oklahoma Press, 1957).

2. Candace Greene and Russell Thornton, eds., *The Year the Stars Fell: Lakota Winter Counts at the Smithsonian* (Washington DC: Smithsonian Institution, 2007). See also Pekka Hämäläinen, *Lakota America: A New History of Indigenous Power* (New Haven, CT: Yale University Press, 2019); Guy Gibbon, *The Sioux: The Dakota and Lakota Nations* (Malden, MA: Wiley-Blackwell, 2002); Royal B. Hassrick, *The Sioux: Life and Customs of a Warrior Society* (Norman: University of Oklahoma Press, 1964).

3. Greene and Thornton, *The Year the Stars Fell*, 173–75. See also Richard White, "The Winning of the West: The Expansion of the Western Sioux in the Eighteenth and Nineteenth Centuries," *Journal of American History* 65 (September 1978): 319–43; Jeffrey Ostler, *The Plains Sioux and U.S. Colonialism from Lewis and Clark to Wounded Knee* (Cambridge: Cambridge University Press, 2004); Anthony R. McGinnis, *Counting Coup and Cutting Horses: Intertribal Warfare on the Northern Plains, 1738–1889* (Lincoln: University of Nebraska Press, 2010).

4. *New York Herald*, November 16, 1877; Utley, *The Lance and the Shield*, 3; Greene and Thornton, *The Year the Stars Fell*, 193–95; differing accounts state that Sitting Bull may have been born in 1831, 1832, 1834, or 1837 near the banks of the Missouri River, the Grand River, the Teton River, or the Yellowstone River. For a genealogical accounting, see LaPointe, *Sitting Bull*, 15–16, 21.

5. Utley, *The Lance and the Shield*, 5–13.

6. Utley, *The Lance and the Shield*, 28–30; Lee Irwin, *The Dream Seekers: Native American Visionary Traditions of the Great Plains* (Norman: University of Oklahoma Press, 1994), 8. See also Raymond J. DeMallie, ed., *The Sixth Grandfather: Black Elk's Teachings Given to John G. Neihardt* (Lincoln: University of Nebraska Press, 1985).

7. Utley, *The Lance and the Shield*, 14–19; Anderson, *Sitting Bull and the Paradox of Lakota Nationhood*, 44–49.

8. Utley, *The Lance and the Shield*, 20–23; LaPointe, *Sitting Bull*, 39–43; Hämäläinen, *Lakota America*, 181.

9. Utley, *The Lance and the Shield*, 26–37; Stanley Vestal, *New Sources of Indian History, 1850–1891* (Norman: University of Oklahoma Press, 1934), 142–52, 270–71. See also Joel W. Martin, *The Land Looks After Us: A History of Native American Religion* (New York: Oxford University Press, 2001).

10. Utley, *The Lance and the Shield*, 31–33; Hämäläinen, *Lakota America*, 103, 173. See also Raymond DeMallie and Douglas R. Parks, eds., *Sioux Indian Religion: Tradition and Innovation* (Norman: University of Oklahoma Press, 1987).

11. Hämäläinen, *Lakota America*, 92–103, 166–69, 191–207. See also Jeffrey Ostler, *The Lakotas and the Black Hills: The Struggle for Sacred Ground* (New York: Penguin Books, 2010).

12. Hämäläinen, *Lakota America*, 215–63; Utley, *The Lance and the Shield*, 38–64; Anderson, *Sitting Bull and the Paradox of Lakota Nationhood*, 11–24, 50.

13. Greene and Thornton, *The Year the Stars Fell*, 255–62; Mark Lee Gardner, *The Earth Is All That Lasts: Crazy Horse, Sitting Bull, and the Last Stand of the Great Sioux Nation* (Boston: Mariner Books, 2022), 83–155.

14. Hämäläinen, *Lakota America*, 290–93. See also Edward Lazarus, *Black Hills, White Justice: The Sioux Nation versus the United States, from 1775 to the Present* (New York: Harper Collins, 1999).

15. Robert Winston Mardock, *The Reformers and the American Indian* (Columbia: University of Missouri Press, 1971), 35–106.

16. Utley, *The Lance and the Shield*, 76–89; Anderson, *Sitting Bull and the Paradox of Lakota Nationhood*, 68–71; Gardner, *The Earth Is All That Lasts*, 140–41; James Macfarlane, "Chief of All the Sioux: An Assessment of Sitting Bull and Lakota Unity, 1868–1876," *American Nineteenth Century History* 11 (Fall 2010): 299–320.

17. *Annual Report of the Commissioner of Indian Affairs to the Secretary of the Interior for the Year 1872* (Washington DC: Government Printing Office, 1872), 456–63; Hämäläinen, *Lakota America*, 322–30; Utley, *The Lance and the Shield*, 90–105.

18. Anderson, *Sitting Bull and the Paradox of Lakota Nationhood*, 83–87. See also M. John Lubetkin, *Jay Cook's Gamble: The Northern Pacific Railroad, the Sioux, and the Panic of 1873* (Norman: University of Oklahoma Press, 2006).

19. Hämäläinen, *Lakota America*, 337–55.

20. Paul A. Hutton, *Phil Sheridan and His Army* (Norman: University of Oklahoma Press, 1999), 282–330.

21. Willis Fletcher Johnson, *The Red Record of the Sioux: Life of Sitting Bull and History of the Indian War of 1890–91* (Philadelphia: Edgewood Publishing, 1891), 192.

22. Utley, *The Lance and the Shield*, 131–37.

23. Utley, *The Lance and the Shield*, 137–39.

24. Hämäläinen, *Lakota America*, 359–71. See also Brad D. Lookingbill, ed., *A Companion to Custer and the Little Bighorn Campaign* (Malden, MA: Wiley-Blackwell, 2015).

25. Utley, *The Lance and the Shield*, 145–64; Anderson, *Sitting Bull and the Paradox of Lakota Nationhood*, 103–9. See also Joseph M. Marshall III, *The Day the World Ended at Little Big Horn: A Lakota History* (New York: Penguin Books, 2008).

26. Interviews and Statements of Chief Henry Oscar One Bull, Walter Stanley Campbell Collection, box 104, folder 11, University of Oklahoma Western History Collections.

27. Gardner, *The Earth Is All That Lasts*, 256–57; Stanley Vestal, "The Works of Sitting Bull: Real and Imaginary," *Southwest Review* 19 (April 1934): 265–78.

28. Hämäläinen, *Lakota America*, 371–73; Utley, *The Lance and the Shield*, 165–73; Robert Wooster, *Nelson A. Miles and the Twilight of the Frontier Army* (Lincoln: University of Nebraska Press, 1993), 76–88.

29. John F. Finerty, *War-Path and Bivouac, or, The Conquest of the Sioux* (Chicago: Donohue Brothers, 1890), 353.

30. Wooster, *Nelson A. Miles and the Twilight of the Frontier Army*, 89–95.

31. Ostler, *The Plains Sioux and U.S. Colonialism*, 66–67; Lazarus, *Black Hills, White Justice*, 90–95.

32. Mark Diedrich, ed., *Sitting Bull: The Collected Speeches* (Rochester, MN: Coyote Books, 1998), 89.

33. Utley, *The Lance and the Shield*, 174–82. See also C. Frank Turner, *Across the Medicine Line: The Epic Confrontation Between Sitting Bull and the North-West Mounted Police* (Toronto: McClelland and Stewart, 1973).

34. Utley, *The Lance and the Shield*, 183–98; Greene and Thornton, *The Year the Stars Fell*, 276.

35. Utley, *The Lance and the Shield*, 199–210. See also Joseph Manzione, *"I Am Looking North for My Life": Sitting Bull, 1876–1881* (Salt Lake City: University of Utah Press, 1991).

36. Joseph M. Marshall III, *The Lakota Way: Stories and Lessons for Living* (New York: Penguin Books, 2001), 216–17. See also Andrew C. Isenberg, *The Destruction of the Bison: An Environmental History, 1750–1920* (New York: Cambridge University Press, 2000).

37. Utley, *The Lance and the Shield*, 211–47; Dennis C. Pope, *Sitting Bull: Prisoner of War* (Pierre: South Dakota Historical Society Press, 2010), 6–36.

38. Pope, *Sitting Bull: Prisoner of War*, 37–121.

39. Gardner, *The Earth Is All That Lasts*, 320–21; Matthew W. Stirling, *Three Pictographic Autobiographies of Sitting Bull*, Smithsonian Miscellaneous Collections, vol. 97, no. 5 (Washington DC: Smithsonian Institution, 1938); Alexis A. Praus, *A New Pictographic Autobiography of Sitting Bull*, Smithsonian Miscellaneous Collections, vol. 123, no. 6 (Washington DC: Smithsonian Institution, 1955); Barbara Risch, "The Picture Changes: Stylistic Variation in Sitting Bull's Biographies," *Great Plains Quarterly* 20 (Fall 2000): 259–80.

40. Utley, *The Lance and the Shield*, 234–52; Lazarus, *Black Hills, White Justice*, 96–118; Vestal, *Sitting Bull*, 256; George E. Hyde, *A Sioux Chronicle* (Norman: University of Oklahoma Press, 1956), 164.

41. Utley, *The Lance and the Shield*, 1–2, 245–71; Vestal, *New Sources of Indian History*, 283. See also Karl van den Broeck, "Everything We Know about Sitting Bull's Crucifix Is Wrong," *True West Magazine*, October 29, 2018, at https://truewestmagazine.com/article/everything-we-know-about-sitting-bulls-crucifix-is-wrong/.

42. Utley, *The Lance and the Shield*, 249–52, 256; LaPointe, *Sitting Bull*, 81, 90; Interviews and Statements of Chief Henry Oscar One Bull, Walter Stanley Campbell Collection, box 104, folder 11, University of Oklahoma Western History Collections.

43. Utley, *The Lance and the Shield*, 260–66; Luther Standing Bear, *My People the Sioux* (Lincoln: University of Nebraska Press, 1975), 184–90. See also Deanne Stillman, *Blood Brothers: The Story of the Strange Friendship between Sitting Bull and Buffalo Bill* (New York: Simon & Schuster, 2017).

44. Utley, *The Lance and the Shield*, 268–83, 290.

45. Ostler, *The Plains Sioux and U.S. Colonialism*, 215; Research Correspondence with A. M. Beede, Fort Yates, North Dakota, Walter Stanley Campbell Collection, box 107, folder 3, University of Oklahoma Western History Collections.

46. Vestal, *New Sources of Indian History*, 92–117; Thomas Augustus Bland, *A Brief History of the Late Military Invasion of the Home of the Sioux* (Washington DC: National Indian Defense Association, 1891), 28–30; Gardner, *The Earth Is All That Lasts*, 341–46, 351–52. See also Eileen Pollack, *Woman Walking Ahead: In Search of Catherine Weldon and Sitting Bull* (Albuquerque: University of New Mexico Press, 2002).

47. Robert Utley, *Last Days of the Sioux Nation* (New Haven, CT: Yale University Press, 1963), 40–83; Rani-Henrik Andersson, *The Lakota Ghost Dance of 1890* (Lincoln: University of Nebraska Press, 2008), 1–29. See also Michael Hittman, *Wovoka and the Ghost Dance* (Lincoln: University of Nebraska Press, 1997).

48. Louis S. Warren, *God's Red Son: The Ghost Dance and the Making of Modern America* (New York: Basic Books, 2017), 170–79, 210–35. See also John Howard Smith, *A Dream of the Judgment Day: American Millennialism and Apocalypticism, 1620–1890* (New York: Oxford University Press, 2021).

49. Utley, *The Lance and the Shield*, 283–90; Andersson, *The Lakota Ghost Dance of 1890*, 31–99; James Mooney, *The Ghost-Dance Religion and the Sioux Outbreak of 1890*, Fourteenth Annual Report of the Bureau of American Ethnology, 1892–93, pt. 2 (Washington DC: Government Printing Office, 1896), 816–54.

50. Anderson, *Sitting Bull and the Paradox of Lakota Nationhood*, 172–80; LaPointe, *Sitting Bull*, 91–93.

51. James McLaughlin, *My Friend the Indian* (New York: Houghton Mifflin, 1910), 185–208; Vestal, *New Sources of Indian History*, 311–12. See also Usher L. Burdick, ed., *My Friend the Indian, or Three Heretofore Unpublished Chapters of the Book Published under the Title My Friend the Indian, by Major James McLaughlin* (Baltimore: Proof Press, 1936).

52. Vestal, *New Sources of Indian History*, 61–72.

53. Gardner, *The Earth Is All That Lasts*, 346–75; LaPointe, *Sitting Bull*, 94–107; Interviews and Statements of Chief Henry Oscar One Bull, Walter Stanley Campbell Collection, box 104, folder 11, University of Oklahoma Western History Collections.

54. Vestal, *New Sources of Indian History*, 1–60; Utley, *The Lance and the Shield*, 291–98.

55. Utley, *The Lance and the Shield*, 298–303. See also John M. Carroll, ed., *The Arrest and Killing of Sitting Bull: A Documentary* (Glendale, CA: Arthur H. Clark, 1986).

56. Greene and Thornton, *The Year the Stars Fell*, 286. See also Joyce M. Szabo, "Mapped Battles and Visual Narratives: The Arrest and Killing of Sitting Bull," *American Indian Art Magazine*, Fall 1996, 64–75.

57. Utley, *The Lance and the Shield*, 303–9; Ostler, *The Plains Sioux and U.S. Colonialism*, 300–326.

58. Hämäläinen, *Lakota America*, 374–82; David W. Grua, *Surviving Wounded Knee: The Lakotas and the Politics of Memory* (New York: Oxford University Press, 2016), 9–29. See also Jerome A. Greene, *American Carnage: Wounded Knee, 1890* (Norman: University of Oklahoma Press, 2014).

59. Gary Clayton Anderson, *Ethnic Cleansing and the Indian: The Crime That Should Haunt America* (Norman: University of Oklahoma Press, 2014), 173–329; Lazarus, *Black Hills, White Justice*, 381–433; *United States v. Sioux Nation of Indians*, 448 U.S. 371 (1980).

60. Utley, *The Lance and the Shield*, 312–14; Anderson, *Sitting Bull and the Paradox of Lakota Nationhood*, 195–96; LaPointe, *Sitting Bull*, 118–27.

61. "Let us put our minds together and see what life we will make for our children," Yanker poster collection, Library of Congress; Marshall III, *The Lakota Way*, 211–20. See also Sitting Bull College at https://www.sittingbull.edu/ (accessed October 14, 2024).

Part 1: Emergence

1. Frances Densmore, *Teton Sioux Music*, Bureau of American Ethnology Bulletin 61 (Washington DC: Government Printing Office, 1918), 63–67; Joseph M. Marshall III, *The Lakota Way: Stories and Lessons for Living* (New York: Penguin, 2001), 16–18, 190–92. At the date of the present writing, Arvol Looking Horse, a Lakota Sioux, is the keeper of the sacred pipe.

2. "Sitting Bull Talks," *New York Herald*, November 16, 1877, pp. 3, 4; W. L. Holloway, ed., *Wild Life on the Plains and Horrors of Indian Warfare* (St. Louis, MO: Pease-Taylor Publishing, 1891), 392–416; Robert M. Utley, *The Lance and the Shield: The Life and Times of Sitting Bull* (New York: Henry Holt, 1993), 3–5, 335.

3. Densmore, *Teton Sioux Music*, 272–73, 460; Stanley Vestal, "The Works of Sitting Bull: Real and Imaginary," *Southwest Review* 19 (April 1934): 265–78; Songs by Sitting Bull, Walter Stanley Campbell Collection, box 104, folder 18, University of Oklahoma Western History Collections.

4. Kimball Pictographic Record No. 1, in Matthew W. Stirling, *Three Pictographic Autobiographies of Sitting Bull*, Smithsonian Miscellaneous Collections, vol. 97, no. 5 (Washington DC: Smithsonian Institution, 1938), 3–34; Reverend John P. Williamson to George Lippitt Andrews, December 12, 1881, Fort Randall Letters Received, Records of the United States Army Continental Commands, 1821–1920, RG 393, National Archives and Records Administration, Washington DC; "Autobiography of Sitting Bull," *New York Herald*, July 7, 1876, p. 3. For a discussion of what "Four Horn's copies" may have meant to the Lakota Sioux, see Candace Greene, "Sitting Bull, Four Horns, and Fort Buford: Questioning A Famous Set of Plains Drawings," *Museum Anthropology Review* 16 (Spring/Fall 2022): 11–29.

5. Stanley Vestal, "Sitting Bull's Maiden Speech," *The Frontier, Magazine of the Northwest* 12 (March 1932): 269–71; Interview of White Bull, Walter Stanley Campbell Collection, box 105, folder 8, University of Oklahoma Western History Collections; G. K. Warren and Engineer Department, United States Army, *Preliminary Report of*

Explorations in Nebraska and Dakota, in the Years 1855–'56–'57, reprint (Washington DC: Government Printing Office, 1875), 18–22, 47–54.

6. Interview of White Bull, Walter Stanley Campbell Collection, box 106, folder 53, University of Oklahoma Western History Collections; Fanny Kelly, *Narrative of My Captivity among the Sioux Indians* (Hartford, CT: Mutual Publishing, 1873); Thomas Augustus Bland, *A Brief History of the Late Military Invasion of the Home of the Sioux* (Washington DC: National Indian Defense Association, 1891), 27–28; Doane Robinson, "The Rescue of Frances Kelly," *South Dakota Historical Collections* 4 (1908): 109–17; Stanley Vestal, *Sitting Bull: Champion of the Sioux*, 2nd ed. (Norman: University of Oklahoma Press, 1957), 62–69.

7. Charles Larpenteur, *Forty Years a Fur Trader on the Upper Missouri, 1833–1872*, vol. II (New York: Francis P. Harper, 1898), 429–30; Mark Lee Gardner, *The Earth Is All That Lasts: Crazy Horse, Sitting Bull, and the Last Stand of the Great Sioux Nation* (Boston: Mariner Books, 2022), 152–53.

8. Joe DeBarthe, *Life and Adventures of Frank Grouard* (St. Joseph, MO: Combe Printing, 1894), 75–83; Gardner, *The Earth Is All That Lasts*, 189–91.

9. Excerpts from G. J. Garraghan, "Father De Smet's Sioux Peace Mission of 1868 and the Journal of Charles Galpin," *Mid-America* 2 (October 1930): 141–63; General Notes by Campbell, Walter Stanley Campbell Collection, box 106, folder 57, University of Oklahoma Western History Collections; Vestal, *Sitting Bull*, 102–8.

10. Eugene Buechel and Paul I. Manhart, *Lakota Tales and Texts*, vol. 2 (Chamberlain, SD: Tipi Press, 1998), 634–43; James Macfarlane, "Chief of All the Sioux: An Assessment of Sitting Bull and Lakota Unity, 1868–1876," *American Nineteenth Century History* 11 (Fall 2010): 299–320; Gary C. Anderson, *Sitting Bull and the Paradox of Lakota Nationhood*, 3rd ed. (New York: Pearson Longman, 2007), 68–71.

11. "A Kind Grandfather," *Talks and Thoughts of the Hampton Indian Students* 15 (January 1902): 1, 3; Candace Greene and Russell Thornton, eds., *The Year the Stars Fell: Lakota Winter Counts at the Smithsonian* (Washington DC: Smithsonian Institution, 2007): 265–69. See also Marshall, *The Lakota Way*.

Part 2: Battleground

1. Smith Pictographic Record No. 16, in Matthew W. Stirling, *Three Pictographic Autobiographies of Sitting Bull*, Smithsonian Miscellaneous Collections, vol. 97, no. 5

(Washington DC: Smithsonian Institution, 1938), 35–48; compare to Pettinger Pictographic Record No. 6 and No. 7, in Stirling, *Three Pictographic Autobiographies of Sitting Bull*, vol. 97, no. 5, 49–57; Robert M. Utley, *The Lance and the Shield: The Life and Times of Sitting Bull* (New York: Henry Holt, 1993), 97–100.

2. MS 1929-b, Sitting Bull pictographic autobiography and related material, National Museum of Natural History, Smithsonian Institution; Stirling, *Three Pictographic Autobiographies of Sitting Bull*, 35–48; Utley, *The Lance and the Shield*, 90–97.

3. Charles A. Eastman, *Indian Heroes and Great Chieftains* (Boston: Little, Brown, 1918), 117–21; Mark Diedrich, ed., *Sitting Bull: The Collected Speeches* (Rochester, MN: Coyote Books, 1998), 75. See also Charles A. Eastman, *In the Beginning, the Sun: The Dakota Legend of Creation* (St. Paul: Minnesota Historical Society Press, 2023).

4. James William Buel, *Heroes of the Plains* (Deposit, NY: Phillips & Burrows, 1886), 572–88; Raymond J. DeMallie, ed., *The Sixth Grandfather: Black Elk's Teachings Given to John G. Neihardt* (Lincoln: University of Nebraska Press, 1985), 163–72; Peter J. Powell, *People of the Sacred Mountain: A History of the Northern Cheyenne Chiefs and Warrior Societies, 1830–1879*, vol. 2 (New York: Harper & Row, 1981), 928–29.

5. John G. Bourke, *On the Border with Crook* (New York: Charles Scribner's Sons, 1891), 241–55; Gary C. Anderson, *Sitting Bull and the Paradox of Lakota Nationhood*, 3rd ed. (New York: Pearson Longman, 2007), 92. Frank Grouard confirmed Sitting Bull's communication in Joe DeBarthe, *Life and Adventures of Frank Grouard* (St. Joseph, MO: Combe Printing, 1894), 173–75, 390.

6. Songs by Sitting Bull, Walter Stanley Campbell Collection, box 104, folder 18, University of Oklahoma Western History Collections; Utley, *The Lance and the Shield*, 144.

7. *New York Herald*, November 16, 1877, p. 3. See also Michael N. Donahue, *Drawing Battle Lines: The Map Testimony of Custer's Last Fight* (El Segundo, CA: Upton & Sons, 2008); Brad D. Lookingbill, ed., *A Companion to Custer and the Little Bighorn Campaign* (Malden, MA: Wiley-Blackwell, 2015).

8. "Sitting Bull Talks," *New York Herald*, November 16, 1877, pp. 3, 4; W. L. Holloway, ed., *Wild Life on the Plains and Horrors of Indian Warfare* (St. Louis, MO: Pease-Taylor Publishing, 1891), 392–416. Compare this interview to a later variant in *New York Times*, May 7, 1881.

9. Buel, *Heroes of the Plains*, 572–58; Diedrich, ed., *Sitting Bull*, 85–86; Ernie LaPointe, *Sitting Bull: His Life and Legacy* (Layton, UT: Gibbs Smith, 2009), 68–72.

10. Man That Smells His Hand to Lt. Col. W. P. Carlin, September 6, 1876, in W. A. Graham, ed., *The Custer Myth: A Source Book of Custerania* (Harrisburg, PA: Stackpole, 1953), 99. Compare this message to prior variants in *St. Paul Pioneer Press*, July 15, 1876, and August 19, 1876; Gary Clayton Anderson, *Ethnic Cleansing and the Indian; The Crime That Should Haunt America* (Norman: University of Oklahoma Press), 303.

11. *Report of the General of the Army*, Annual Report of the U.S. Secretary of War (Washington DC: Government Printing Office, 1876), 482–87, 516–17; Utley, *The Lance and the Shield*, 168–70.

12. Life of Sitting Bull by White Bull, Walter Stanley Campbell Collection, box 105, folder 4, University of Oklahoma Western History Collections; Continuation of Interview of White Bull, Walter Stanley Campbell Collection, box 105, folder 24, University of Oklahoma Western History Collections; Stanley Vestal, *Sitting Bull: Champion of the Sioux*, 2nd ed. (Norman: University of Oklahoma Press, 1957), 193–202. See also Robert Wooster, *Nelson A. Miles and the Twilight of the Frontier Army* (Lincoln: University of Nebraska Press, 1993).

Part 3: Border Crossings

1. "Abbot Marty Visits Sitting Bull," *Annals of the Catholic Indian Missions of America* 2 (January 1878): 7–10; *Bismarck Tri-Weekly Tribune*, June 15, 1877; Mark Diedrich, ed., *Sitting Bull: The Collected Speeches* (Rochester, MN: Coyote Books, 1998), 97–100.

2. *Report of the Sitting Bull Indian Commission* (Washington DC: Government Printing Office, 1877), 3–9; Gary C. Anderson, *Sitting Bull and the Paradox of Lakota Nationhood*, 3rd ed. (New York: Pearson Longman, 2007), 127–29.

3. James Walsh to Assistant Commissioner, March 24, 1879, James Walsh Papers, Provincial Archives of Manitoba, quoted in Diedrich, *Sitting Bull*, 115; C. Frank Turner, *Across the Medicine Line: The Epic Confrontation Between Sitting Bull and the North-West Mounted Police* (Toronto: McClelland and Stewart, 1973), 163–65; Joseph Manzione, *"I Am Looking North for My Life": Sitting Bull, 1876–1881* (Salt Lake: University of Utah Press, 1991), 133–34.

4. *Chicago Daily Tribune*, July 5, 1879; Lewis O. Saum, "Stanley Huntley Interviews Sitting Bull: Event, Pseudo-Event, or Fabrication?" *Montana: The Magazine of Western History* 32 (Spring 1982): 2–15.

5. Smith Pictographic Record No. 15, in Matthew W. Stirling, *Three Pictographic Autobiographies of Sitting Bull*, Smithsonian Miscellaneous Collections, vol. 97, no. 5 (Washington DC: Smithsonian Institution, 1938), 35–48; compare to Pettinger Pictographic Record No. 10, in Stirling, *Three Pictographic Autobiographies of Sitting Bull*, vol. 97, no. 5, 49–57. See also Robert M. Utley, *The Last Sovereigns: Sitting Bull and the Resistance of the Free Lakota* (Lincoln: University of Nebraska Press, 2020), 65–72.

6. Photograph of Buffalo Robe Painting by Sitting Bull, MacKenzie Art Gallery, https://mackenzie.art/sitting-bull-tatanka-iyotake/ (accessed October 14, 2024); Tatanka Iyotake (Sitting Bull), "Buffalo Robe," circa 1877–1881, pigment on American bison hide, State Historical Society of North Dakota, # 10117; Utley, *The Last Sovereigns*, 59–105.

7. "Tatonca 'O Tocha Talks," *St. Paul and Minneapolis Pioneer Press*, July 21, 1881; T. M. Newson, *Thrilling Scenes among the Indians* (Chicago: Donohue, Henneberry, 1890), 181–83; Utley, *The Last Sovereigns*, 107–20.

8. "A Chat with the Chief," *St. Paul and Minneapolis Pioneer Press*, August 4, 1881; Robert M. Utley, *The Lance and the Shield: The Life and Times of Sitting Bull* (New York: Henry Holt, 1993), 236–41.

9. Willis Fletcher Johnson, *The Red Record of the Sioux: Life of Sitting Bull and History of the Indian War of 1890–1891* (Philadelphia, PA: Edgewood Publishing, 1891), 162–67; Diedrich, ed., *Sitting Bull*, 142. See also *Philadelphia Evening Telegraph*, September 6, 1881.

10. James Creelman, *On the Great Highway* (Boston: Lothrop, Lee & Shepard, 1901), 297–302; Dennis C. Pope, *Sitting Bull, Prisoner of War* (Pierre: South Dakota Historical Society Press, 2010), 42–122.

11. Typescript Excerpts from Published Sources regarding Sitting Bull, Walter Stanley Campbell Collection, box 113, folder 9, University of Oklahoma Western History Collections; Rudolf Cronau, "My Visit among the Hostile Dakota Indians and How They Became My Friends," *South Dakota Historical Collections* 22 (1946): 410–25; Pope, *Sitting Bull, Prisoner of War*, 60–67.

12. Sitting Bull Speech to Walking Elk, Letter to George Lippitt Andrews, December 3, 1881, Fort Randall Letters Received, Records of the United States Army Continental Commands, 1821–1920, RG 393, National Archives and Records Administration, Washington DC; Pope, *Sitting Bull*, 42–127.

Part 4: Standing Rock

1. "Revised Standing Rock," *St. Paul and Minneapolis Pioneer Press*, May 26, 1883, p. 9; Stanley Vestal, *New Sources of Indian History* (Norman: University of Oklahoma Press, 1934), 290–95; Dennis C. Pope, *Sitting Bull, Prisoner of War* (Pierre: South Dakota Historical Society Press, 2010), 128–35.

2. S. Rep., 48th Cong., 1st Sess., no. 283, serial 2164 (1883), at 71–82; Colin G. Calloway, ed., *Our Hearts Fell to the Ground: Plains Indian Views of How the West Was Lost*, 2nd ed. (Boston: Bedford/St. Martin's, 2018), 148–50; Robert M. Utley, *The Lance and the Shield: The Life and Times of Sitting Bull* (New York: Henry Holt, 1993), 248–59.

3. Typescript Accounts regarding the Life of Sitting Bull, Walter Stanley Campbell Collection, box 104, folder 21, University of Oklahoma Western History Collections; Vestal, *New Sources of Indian History*, 274–75; W. C. Vanderwerth, *Indian Oratory: Famous Speeches by Noted Indian Chieftains* (Norman: University of Oklahoma Press, 1971), 189.

4. Quotations from newspaper snippets appear in Mark Diedrich and Paul D. Nelson, "Sitting Bull and His 1884 Visit to St. Paul: 'A Shady Pair' and an 'Attempt on His Life,'" *Ramsey County History* 38 (Spring 2003): 4–12; Mark Diedrich, ed., *Sitting Bull: The Collected Speeches* (Rochester, MN: Coyote Books, 1998), 154; Utley, *The Lance and the Shield*, 260–62.

5. Luther Standing Bear, *My People the Sioux* (Lincoln: University of Nebraska Press, 1975), 185–87; Utley, *The Lance and the Shield*, 262–64.

6. *The Globe* (Toronto), August 24, 1885; *Evening Journal* (Detroit), September 5, 1885; *Evening Leader* (Grand Rapids), September 12, 1885; *St. Louis Globe Democrat*, October 3, 1885; Typescript Excerpts from Interviews with Sitting Bull, Walter Stanley Campbell Collection, box 113, folder 7, University of Oklahoma Western History Collections. See also Joy S. Kasson, *Buffalo Bill's Wild West: Celebrity, Memory, and Popular History* (New York: Hill and Wang, 2000).

7. Sitting Bull, Letter "To My Great Father," Washington DC, June 23, 1885, File 1885-14386, Letters Received, 1881–1907, Entry PI-163 91, Record Group 75, Records of the Bureau of Indian Affairs, National Archives and Records Administration; *Washington Post*, June 24, 1885; Diedrich, ed., *Sitting Bull*, 158, 160, 162; Utley, *The Lance and the Shield*, 265–66.

8. Sitting Bull Illustrates to the Silent Eaters of the Way the Indians Tried to Stand In with the Indian Agent, Walter Stanley Campbell Collection, Box 104, Folder 21, University of Oklahoma Western History Collections; Vestal, *New Sources of Indian History*, 279–80; Diedrich, *Sitting Bull*, 164.

9. *Washington Post*, October 16, 1888; Diedrich, *Sitting Bull*, 170; Utley, *The Lance and the Shield*, 268–77.

10. US commissioners and delegations of Sioux chiefs visiting Washington, October 13, 1888, Prints and Photographs Division, Library of Congress; Stanley Vestal, *Sitting Bull: Champion of the Sioux*, 2nd ed. (Norman: University of Oklahoma Press, 1957), 256–62. See also Frank H. Goodyear III, "Wanted: Sitting Bull and His Photographic Portrait," *South Dakota History* 40 (Summer 2010): 136–62.

11. Sitting Bull's Address to the Silent Eaters Protesting the Treaty of 1889, Walter Stanley Campbell Collection, box 104, folder 21, University of Oklahoma Western History Collections; Vestal, *New Sources of Indian History*, 303–4; Utley, *The Lance and the Shield*, 277–80.

12. James McLaughlin to Commissioner of Indian Affairs, Standing Rock Agency, November 19, 1890, in Typescript Research Correspondence regarding the Death of Sitting Bull, Walter Stanley Campbell Collection, box 114, folder 6, University of Oklahoma Western History Collections; James McLaughlin, *My Friend the Indian* (New York: Houghton Mifflin, 1910), 190–208; Rani-Henrik Andersson, *The Lakota Ghost Dance of 1890* (Lincoln: University of Nebraska Press, 2008), 1–127. See also Usher L. Burdick, ed., *My Friend the Indian, or Three Heretofore Unpublished Chapters of the Book Published Under the Title My Friend the Indian, by Major James McLaughlin* (Baltimore: Proof Press, 1936).

13. Fox Letter, in Typescript Research Correspondence regarding the Death of Sitting Bull, Walter Stanley Campbell Collection, box 114, folder 6, University of Oklahoma Western History Collections; Vestal, *Sitting Bull*, 282–85; Utley, *The Lance and the Shield*, 293–307.

Postscript: Something Said in Passing

1. Quotations from newspaper excerpts appear in Willis Fletcher Johnson, *The Red Record of the Sioux: Life of Sitting Bull and History of the Indian War of 1890–91* (Philadelphia: Edgewood Publishing, 1891), 194–203; Thomas Augustus Bland, *A Brief History of the Late Military Invasion of the Home of the Sioux* (Washington DC: National Indian Defense Association, 1891), 24–27; Stanley Vestal, *New Sources of Indian History, 1850–1891* (Norman: University of Oklahoma Press, 1934), 90–92; Lee Miller, ed., *From the Heart: Voices of the American Indian* (New York: Alfred A. Knopf, 1995), 251–54.

QUESTIONS FOR DISCUSSION

Questions about Emergence

1.1: What early conceptions about the "whites" were shared by Sitting Bull?

1.2: How did the Lakota Sioux acquire food, clothing, and shelter around the mid-1800s?

1.3: Why did the Lakota count coups upon their enemies?

1.4: What made Sitting Bull influential in tribal councils?

1.5: To what extent were the Hunkpapa receptive to the policies of the United States?

Questions about Battleground

2.1: What issues led to war between the United States and the Lakota Sioux?

2.2: Where did Sitting Bull hunt for game during the early 1870s?

2.3: What was Sitting Bull's position regarding the ownership of the Black Hills?

2.4: How did the Lakota and their allies prevail in battle at the Little Bighorn River?

2.5: Why did Sitting Bull want to talk to the "Man with the Bear Coat"?

Questions about Border Crossings

3.1: When did the free Lakota decide to camp in the Dominion of Canada?

3.2: Why were so many individuals drawn to Sitting Bull's campsite north of the 49th parallel?

3.3: How did the United States put pressure on Sitting Bull from across the border?

3.4: What made Sitting Bull return to the United States in 1881?

3.5: In what ways did the US government punish the prisoners of war?

Questions about Standing Rock

4.1: How did settler sovereignty impact the reservation system of the United States?

4.2: To what extent did Sitting Bull's role in traveling showcases suggest adaptiveness?

4.3: What did Sitting Bull mean when he said that "someday my children will be educated"?

4.4: What evidence indicates that Lakota spiritualism complemented the Ghost Dance in 1890?

4.5: Who was responsible for the death of Sitting Bull?

Glossary

akicitas: warriors or camp police.

allotment: a plot of land from communal holdings distributed to an individual or a family.

assimilation: the process for integrating ethnic populations into a society.

bison: a large bovine species; colloquially known as buffaloes.

blotáhunka: war chief.

Buffalo Bill's Wild West: a traveling vaudevillian show organized by William F. Cody.

calumet: a ceremonial pipe used by Native Americans.

cankukomnipi: a game.

canku wakán: a sacred road.

Carlisle Indian Industrial School: an off-reservation Indian boarding school located in Carlisle, Pennsylvania, where it operated from 1879 to 1918.

ceska maza: reservation police units.

commission: an official body of people with assigned responsibility to do something, usually for a government.

Corps of Discovery: the military expedition of Captain Meriwether Lewis and Lieutenant William Clark from 1804 to 1806.

coup: a war honor.

epidemic: the appearance of a particular disease in a large number of people at the same time.

ethnic cleansing: a widespread, systematic assault directed against a stateless group with durable claims to an ancestral homeland.

Fort Laramie Treaty: the 1868 agreement between the United States and the Lakota Sioux.

fur trade: a worldwide industry dealing in the acquisition and sale of animal pelts.

Ghost Dance: a pan-Indian movement originating in 1889.

Grattan Fight: occurring on August 19, 1854, the incident led to conflict between the United States Army and Lakota Sioux warriors.

Great American Desert: an inhospitable landscape, which early-nineteenth-century maps located between the Mississippi River and Rocky Mountains.

hanblecheyapi: a vision quest.

heyoka: a strange and wondrous human being.

hochoka: a camp circle.

hóka hé: a battle cry.

Horse Creek Treaty: the 1851 agreement between the United States and Plains Indians; also called the first Fort Laramie Treaty.

Indian country: lands reserved by the federal government for Native American usage.

Indian removal: policy of forced relocation for tribal groups to Indian Territory.

Indian Rights Association: a nongovernmental organization promoting the acculturation of Native Americans after 1882.

inikagapi: a sweat lodge.

itancan: chief of a band.

Lakota: allied western Sioux; also called Tetons.

Long Knives: slang for non-Indian invaders.

Louisiana Purchase: the 1803 acquisition of interior borderland territory by the United States from France.

Manifest Destiny: a nationalistic assumption that the United States was ordained by God and history to expand its dominion westward across the North American continent.

Métis: Canadian populations of mixed European and Indigenous ancestry.

millenarianism: a Christian belief in the coming of a new age.

mitakuye oyasin: a Siouxan expression regarding kinship and tribal relations.

Mounties: North-West Mounted Police in the Dominion of Canada.

Glossary 173

National Indian Defense Association: a nongovernmental organization upholding Native American land claims after 1885.

Northern Pacific Railway: a transcontinental railroad built from 1870 to 1883.

Očhéthi Šakówiŋ: the Seven Council Fires of the Sioux.

ohunkakan: folktales.

oyáte: a distinct people or tribal band.

Pahá Sápa: Black Hills.

Panic of 1873: a financial crisis that initiated an economic depression in the United States.

peace policy: a governmental effort to place humanitarian reformers in charge of the reservation system and to discourage armed conflicts with tribal groups.

reservation: a circumscribed area of public lands reserved for Indigenes.

settler sovereignty: the government-sponsored empowerment of colonizers against Indigenes.

Shirt Wearers: distinguished figures within a particular Lakota community.

Sioux: an ethnic cluster of Native Americans or their linguistic family.

Slota: roving Métis Canadian traders.

smallpox: a contagious viral disease.

tiospayes: a collection of lodges.

United States v. Sioux Nation of Indians: the 1980 Supreme Court case that adjudicated the federal government's seizure of the Black Hills from the Lakota.

vanishing race: a popularized concept regarding the disappearance of Native Americans in the United States.

Wakantanka: the Great Mysterious One or the Great Spirit.

wakicunza: honored administrator.

wanagi wachipi ki: the spirit dance.

wasi'chus: non-Indian people of western European descent.

wichásha wakán: holy man.

winter counts: pictorial calendars or histories.

witko: a fool.

wiwáŋyaŋg wachipi: sun dancing.

wotawe: a medicine bundle.

Yellowstone National Park: America's first national park, established by the United States in 1872.

Selected Bibliography

"Abbot Marty Visits Sitting Bull." *Annals of the Catholic Indian Missions of America* 2 (January 1878): 7–10.

Adams, Alexander B. *Sitting Bull: An Epic of the Plains.* New York: G. P. Putnam's Sons, 1973.

Allison, Edward H. "Sitting Bull's Birthplace." *South Dakota Historical Collections* 6 (1912): 270–72.

Allison, Edward H. *The Surrender of Sitting Bull.* Dayton, OH: Walker Lithograph and Printing, 1891.

Anderson, Gary C. *Ethnic Cleansing and the Indian: The Crime That Should Haunt America.* Norman: University of Oklahoma Press, 2014.

Anderson, Gary C. *Sitting Bull and the Paradox of Lakota Nationhood.* 3rd ed. New York: Pearson Longman, 2007.

Andersson, Rani-Henrik. *The Lakota Ghost Dance of 1890.* Lincoln: University of Nebraska Press, 2008.

Andersson, Rani-Henrik. *A Whirlwind Passed through Our Country: Lakota Voices of the Ghost Dance.* Norman: University of Oklahoma, 2018.

Armstrong, Virginia, ed. *I Have Spoken: American History through the Voices of the Indians.* Chicago: Sage Books, 1971.

Barrett, Carole. "One Bull: A Man of Good Understanding." *North Dakota History* 66 (Summer 1999): 3–16.

Beck, Paul N. *Columns of Vengeance: Soldiers, Sioux, and the Punitive Expeditions, 1863–1864.* Norman: University of Oklahoma Press, 2013.

Beede, A. McG. (Aaron McGaffey). *Sitting Bull—Custer.* Bismarck, ND: Bismarck Tribune, 1913.

Berthrong, Donald J. "Walter Stanley Campbell: Plainsman." *Arizona and the West* 7 (Summer, 1965): 91–104.

Blackhawk, Ned. *The Rediscovery of America: Native Peoples and the Unmaking of U.S. History.* New Haven, CT: Yale University Press, 2023.

Blaisdell, Bob, ed. *Great Speeches by Native Americans.* Mineola, NY: Dover, 2000.

Bland, Thomas Augustus. *A Brief History of the Late Military Invasion of the Home of the Sioux.* Washington DC: National Indian Defense Association, 1891.

Bourke, John G. *On the Border with Crook.* New York: Charles Scribner's Sons, 1891.

Buchholtz, Debra. *The Battle of the Greasy Grass/Little Bighorn: Custer's Last Stand in Memory, History, and Popular Culture.* New York: Routledge Press, 2012.

Buechel, Eugene, and Paul I. Manhart. *Lakota Tales and Texts.* 2 vols. Chamberlain, SD: Tipi Press, 1998.

Buel, James William. *Heroes of the Plains.* Deposit, NY: Phillips & Burrows, 1886.

Burdick, Usher L., ed. *My Friend the Indian, or Three Heretofore Unpublished Chapters of the Book Published Under the Title My Friend the Indian, by Major James McLaughlin.* Baltimore: Proof Press, 1936.

Calloway, Colin G. *First Peoples: A Documentary Survey of American Indian History.* 6th ed. Boston: Bedford/St. Martin's, 2019.

Calloway, Colin G., ed. *Our Hearts Fell to the Ground: Plains Indian Views of How the West Was Lost.* 2nd ed. Boston: Bedford/St. Martin's, 2018.

Carroll, John M., ed. *The Arrest and Killing of Sitting Bull: A Documentary.* Glendale, CA: Arthur H. Clark, 1986.

Clodfelter, Michael. *The Dakota War: The United States Army Versus the Sioux, 1862–1865.* Jefferson, NC: McFarland, 1998.

Creelman, James. *On the Great Highway.* Boston: Lothrop, Lee & Shepard, 1901.

Cronau, Rudolf. "My Visit among the Hostile Dakota Indians and How They Became My Friends." *South Dakota Historical Collections* 22 (1946): 410–25.

DeBarthe, Joe. *Life and Adventures of Frank Grouard.* St. Joseph, MO: Combe Printing, 1894.

Deloria, Vine, Jr. *God Is Red: A Native View of Religion.* New York: Putnam, 1973.

DeMallie, Raymond J., ed. *The Sixth Grandfather: Black Elk's Teachings Given to John G. Neihardt.* Lincoln: University of Nebraska Press, 1985.

DeMallie, Raymond J., and Douglas R. Parks, eds. *Sioux Indian Religion: Tradition and Innovation.* Norman: University of Oklahoma Press, 1987.

DeMallie, Raymond J., and Vine Deloria Jr., eds. *Documents of American Indian Diplomacy: Treaties, Agreements and Conventions 1775–1979.* 2 vols. Norman: University of Oklahoma Press, 1999.

DeMallie, Raymond J., and Vine Deloria Jr., eds. *Proceedings of the Great Peace Commission of 1867–1868.* Washington DC: Institute for the Development of Indian Law, 1975.

Densmore, Frances. *Teton Sioux Music.* Bureau of American Ethnology Bulletin 61. Washington DC: Government Printing Office, 1918.

Dickson, Ephriam, III, ed. *Sitting Bull Surrender Census.* Pierre: South Dakota State Historical Society Press, 2010.

Diedrich, Mark, ed. *Sitting Bull: The Collected Speeches.* Rochester, MN: Coyote Books, 1998.

Diedrich, Mark, and Paul D. Nelson. "Sitting Bull and His 1884 Visit to St. Paul: 'A Shady Pair' and an 'Attempt on His Life.'" *Ramsey County History* 38 (Spring 2003): 4–12.

Diessner, Don. *There Are No Indians Left But Me! Sitting Bull's Story.* El Segundo, CA: Upton & Sons, 1993.

Donahue, Michael N. *Drawing Battle Lines: The Map Testimony of Custer's Last Fight.* El Segundo, CA: Upton & Sons, 2008.

Dunbar-Ortiz, Roxanne. *An Indigenous Peoples' History of the United States*. Boston: Beacon Press, 2014.

Dunlay, Thomas W. *Wolves for the Blue Soldiers: Indian Scouts and Auxiliaries with the United States Army, 1860–1890*. Lincoln: University of Nebraska Press, 1987.

Finerty, John F. *War-Path and Bivouac, or, The Conquest of the Sioux*. Chicago: Donohue Brothers, 1890.

Eastman, Charles A. *Indian Boyhood*. Boston: Little, Brown, 1902.

Eastman, Charles A. *Indian Heroes and Great Chieftains*. Boston: Little, Brown, 1918.

Eastman, Charles A. *In the Beginning, the Sun: The Dakota Legend of Creation*. Edited by Sydney Beane and Gail Johnsen. St. Paul: Minnesota Historical Society Press, 2023.

Estes, Nick. *Our History Is the Future: Standing Rock Versus the Dakota Access Pipeline, and the Long Tradition of Indigenous Resistance*. New York: Verso, 2019.

Gardner, Mark Lee. *The Earth Is All That Lasts: Crazy Horse, Sitting Bull, and the Last Stand of the Great Sioux Nation*. Boston: Mariner Books, 2022.

Garland, Hamlin. *The Book of the American Indian*. New York: Harper Brothers, 1923.

Garraghan, G. J. "Father De Smet's Sioux Peace Mission of 1868 and the Journal of Charles Galpin." *Mid-America* 2 (October 1930): 141–63.

Genetin-Pilawa, C. Joseph. *Crooked Paths to Allotment: The Fight over Federal Indian Policy after the Civil War*. Chapel Hill: University of North Carolina Press, 2012.

Gibbon, Guy. *The Sioux: The Dakota and Lakota Nations*. Malden, MA: Wiley-Blackwell, 2002.

Goodyear, Frank H., III. "Wanted: Sitting Bull and His Photographic Portrait." *South Dakota History* 40 (Summer 2010): 136–62.

Graham, W. A., ed. *The Custer Myth: A Source Book of Custerania*. Harrisburg, PA: Stackpole, 1953.

Gray, John S. *Centennial Campaign: The Sioux War of 1876*. Reprint. Norman: University of Oklahoma Press, 1988.

Greene, Candace. "Sitting Bull, Four Horns, and Fort Buford: Questioning a Famous Set of Plains Drawings." *Museum Anthropology Review* 16 (Spring/Fall 2022): 11–29.

Greene, Candace. "Verbal Meets Visual: Sitting Bull and the Representation of History." *Ethnohistory* 62 (April 2015): 217–40.

Greene, Candace, and Russell Thornton, eds. *The Year the Stars Fell: Lakota Winter Counts at the Smithsonian*. Washington DC: Smithsonian Institution, 2007.

Greene, Jerome A. *American Carnage: Wounded Knee, 1890*. Norman: University of Oklahoma Press, 2014.

Greene, Jerome A. *Battles and Skirmishes of the Great Sioux War, 1876–1877*. Norman: University of Oklahoma Press, 1996.

Greene, Jerome A., ed. *Lakota and Cheyenne: Indian Views of the Great Sioux War*. Norman: University of Oklahoma Press, 2000.

Greene, Jerome A. *Stricken Field: The Little Bighorn since 1876*. Norman: University of Oklahoma Press, 2020.

Greene, Jerome A. *Yellowstone Command: Colonel Nelson A. Miles and the Great Sioux War, 1876–1877*. Lincoln: University of Nebraska Press, 1991.

Grua, David W. *Surviving Wounded Knee: The Lakotas and the Politics of Memory*. New York: Oxford University Press, 2016.

Gump, James O. *The Dust Rose Like Smoke: The Subjugation of the Zulu and the Sioux*. Lincoln: University of Nebraska Press, 1994.

Hämäläinen, Pekka. *Lakota America: A New History of Indigenous Power*. New Haven, CT: Yale University Press, 2019.

Hammer, Kenneth, ed. *Custer in '76: Walter Camp's Notes on the Custer Fight*. Reprint. Norman: University of Oklahoma Press, 1990.

Hardorff, Richard, ed. *Lakota Recollections of the Custer Fight*. Lincoln: University of Nebraska Press, 1997.

Hassrick, Royal B. *The Sioux: Life and Customs of a Warrior Society*. Norman: University of Oklahoma Press, 1964.

Hedren, Paul L. *Great Sioux War Orders of Battle: How the United States Army Waged War on the Northern Plains, 1876–1877*. Norman: University of Oklahoma Press, 2011.

Hittman, Michael. *Wovoka and the Ghost Dance*. Lincoln: University of Nebraska Press, 1997.

Holder, Preston. *The Hoe and the Horse on the Plains: A Study of Cultural Development among North American Indians*. Lincoln: University of Nebraska Press, 1974.

Holloway, W. L., ed. *Wild Life on the Plains and Horrors of Indian Warfare*. St. Louis, MO: Pease-Taylor Publishing, 1891.

Hoover, Herbert T. *The Sioux Agreement of 1889 and Its Aftermath*. Pierre: South Dakota Historical Society, 1989.

Howard, James H. "Plains Indian Feathered Bonnets." *Plains Anthropologist* 1 (December 1954): 23–26.

Hoxie, Frederick. *A Final Promise: The Campaign to Assimilate the Indians, 1880–1920*. Lincoln: University of Nebraska Press, 2001.

Hoxie, Frederick, ed. *Talking Back to Civilization: Indian Voices from the Progressive Era*. Boston: Bedford/St. Martin's, 2001.

Hutton, Paul A. *Phil Sheridan and His Army*. Norman: University of Oklahoma Press, 1999.

Hyde, George E. *A Sioux Chronicle*. Norman: University of Oklahoma Press, 1956.

Hyde, George E. *Spotted Tail's Folk: A History of the Brule Sioux*. Norman: University of Oklahoma Press, 1974.

Irwin, Lee. *The Dream Seekers: Native American Visionary Traditions of the Great Plains*. Norman: University of Oklahoma Press, 1994.

Isenberg, Andrew C. *The Destruction of the Bison: An Environmental History, 1750–1920*. New York: Cambridge University Press, 2000.

Jackson, Donald. *Custer's Gold*. New Haven, CT: Yale University Press, 1966.

Jackson, Helen Hunt. *A Century of Dishonor: A Sketch of the United States Government's Dealings with Some of the Indian Tribes*. New York: Harper Brothers, 1881.

Johnson, Willis Fletcher. *The Red Record of the Sioux: Life of Sitting Bull and History of the Indian War of 1890–91*. Philadelphia: Edgewood Publishing, 1891.

Kasson, Joy S. *Buffalo Bill's Wild West: Celebrity, Memory, and Popular History*. New York: Hill and Wang, 2000.

Kelly, Fanny. *Narrative of My Captivity Among the Sioux Indians*. Hartford, CT: Mutual Publishing, 1873.

"A Kind Grandfather." *Talks and Thoughts of the Hampton Indian Students* 15 (January 1902): 1, 3.

Klein, Kerwin Lee. *Frontiers of Historical Imagination: Narrating the European Conquest of Native America, 1890–1990*. Berkeley: University of California Press, 1997.

LaPointe, Ernie. *Sitting Bull: His Life and Legacy*. Layton, UT: Gibbs Smith, 2009.

Larpenteur, Charles. *Forty Years a Fur Trader on the Upper Missouri, 1833–1872*. Vol. 2. New York: Francis P. Harper, 1898.

Larson, Robert W. *Gall: Lakota War Chief*. Norman: University of Oklahoma Press, 2009.

Larson, Robert W. *Red Cloud: Warrior-Statesman of the Lakota Sioux*. Norman: University of Oklahoma Press, 1997.

Lazarus, Edward. *Black Hills, White Justice: The Sioux Nation versus the United States, From 1775 to the Present*. New York: HarperCollins, 1991.

Lehman, Tim. *Bloodshed at Little Bighorn: Sitting Bull, Custer, and the Destinies of Nations*. Baltimore, MD: Johns Hopkins University Press, 2010.

Lookingbill, Brad D., ed. *A Companion to Custer and the Little Bighorn Campaign*. Malden, MA: Wiley-Blackwell, 2015.

Lubetkin, M. John, ed. *Before Custer: Surveying the Yellowstone, 1872*. Norman: University of Oklahoma Press, 2015.

Lubetkin, M. John, ed. *Custer and the 1873 Yellowstone Survey: A Documentary History*. Norman: University of Oklahoma Press, 2013.

Lubetkin, M. John. *Jay Cook's Gamble: The Northern Pacific Railroad, the Sioux, and the Panic of 1873*. Norman: University of Oklahoma Press, 2006.

Macfarlane, James. "Chief of All the Sioux: An Assessment of Sitting Bull and Lakota Unity, 1868–1876." *American Nineteenth Century History* 11 (Fall 2010): 299–320.

Maddra, Sam A. *Hostiles? The Lakota Ghost Dance and Buffalo Bill's Wild West*. Norman: University of Oklahoma Press, 2006.

Mallery, Garrick. *Picture Writing of the American Indians*. 2 vols. Reprint. New York: Dover Books, 1972.

Mann, Michael. *The Dark Side of Democracy: Explaining Ethnic Cleansing*. New York: Cambridge University Press, 2005.

Manzione, Joseph. *"I Am Looking North for My Life": Sitting Bull, 1876–1881*. Salt Lake: University of Utah Press, 1991.

Mardock, Robert Winston. *The Reformers and the American Indian*. Columbia: University of Missouri Press, 1971.

Marquis, Thomas B. *Wooden Leg: A Warrior Who Fought Custer*. Minneapolis, MN: Midwest Company, 1931.

Marshall, Joseph M., III. *The Day the World Ended at Little Bighorn: A Lakota History*. New York: Penguin, 2008.

Marshall, Joseph M., III. *The Lakota Way: Stories and Lessons for Living*. New York: Penguin, 2001.

Martin, Joel W. *The Land Looks After Us: A History of Native American Religion*. New York: Oxford University Press, 2001.

Matteoni, Norman E. *Prairie Man: The Struggle between Sitting Bull and Indian Agent James McLaughlin*. Guilford, CT: Two Dot, 2015.

McChristian, Douglas C. *Regular Army O!: Soldiering on the Western Frontier, 1865–1891*. Norman: University of Oklahoma Press, 2017.

McGinnis, Anthony R. *Counting Coup and Cutting Horses: Intertribal Warfare on the Northern Plains, 1738–1889*. Lincoln: University of Nebraska Press, 2010.

McLaughlin, Castle, ed. *A Lakota War Book from the Little Bighorn: The Pictographic Autobiography of Half Moon*. Cambridge, MA: Peabody Museum Press, 2013.

McLaughlin, James. *My Friend the Indian*. New York: Houghton Mifflin, 1910.

Means, Jeffrey D. "'Indians Shall Do Things in Common': Oglala Lakota Identity and Cattle Raising on the Pine Ridge Reservation." *Montana: The Magazine of Western History* 61 (Autumn 2011): 9–15.

Michno, Gregory F. *Lakota Noon: The Indian Narrative of Custer's Defeat*. Missoula, MT: Mountain Press Publishing, 1997.

Miller, David Humphreys. *Custer's Fall: The Indian Side of the Story*. New York: Duell, Sloan and Pearce, 1957.

Miller, Lee, ed. *From the Heart: Voices of the American Indian*. New York: Alfred A. Knopf, 1995.

Milligan, Edward A. *Dakota Twilight: The Standing Rock Sioux, 1874–1890*. Hicksville, NY: Exposition Press, 1976.

Mooney, James. *The Ghost-Dance Religion and the Sioux Outbreak of 1890*. Fourteenth Annual Report of the Bureau of American Ethnology, 1892–93, Pt. 2. Washington DC: Government Printing Office, 1896.

Moses, L. G. *Wild West Shows and the Images of American Indians, 1883–1933*. Albuquerque: University of New Mexico Press, 1996.

Murphy, Emmett C., with Michael Snell. *The Genius of Sitting Bull: Thirteen Heroic Strategies for Today's Business Leaders*. Upper Saddle River, NJ: Prentice Hall, 1992.

Neihardt, John G., and Black Elk. *Black Elk Speaks: Being the Life Story of a Holy Man of the Oglala Sioux*. Lincoln: University of Nebraska Press, 1961.

Newson, T. M. *Thrilling Scenes among the Indians*. Chicago: Donohue, Henneberry, 1890.

Ostler, Jeffrey. *The Lakotas and the Black Hills: The Struggle for Sacred Ground*. New York: Penguin, 2010.

Ostler, Jeffrey. *The Plains Sioux and U.S. Colonialism from Lewis and Clark to Wounded Knee*. Cambridge: Cambridge University Press, 2004.

Philbrick, Nathaniel. *The Last Stand: Custer, Sitting Bull, and the Battle of the Little Bighorn*. New York: Penguin, 2011.

Pollack, Eileen. *Woman Walking Ahead: In Search of Catherine Weldon and Sitting Bull*. Albuquerque: University of New Mexico Press, 2002.

Pope, Dennis C. *Sitting Bull, Prisoner of War*. Pierre: South Dakota Historical Society Press, 2010.

Porte Crayon [pseud.]. "Sitting Bull—Autobiography of the Famous Sioux Chief." *Harpers Weekly*, July 29, 1876.

Powell, Peter J. *People of the Sacred Mountain: A History of the Northern Cheyenne Chiefs and Warrior Societies, 1830–1879*. Vol. 2. New York: Harper & Row, 1981.

Praus, Alexis A. *A New Pictographic Autobiography of Sitting Bull*. Smithsonian Miscellaneous Collections, vol. 123, no. 6. Washington DC: Smithsonian Institution, 1955.

Prucha, Francis Paul. *The Great Father: The United States Government and the American Indians*. 2 vols. Lincoln: University of Nebraska Press, 1984.

Report of the Sitting Bull Indian Commission. Washington DC: Government Printing Office, 1877.

Richardson, Heather Cox. *West from Appomattox: The Reconstruction of America after the Civil War*. New Haven, CT: Yale University Press, 2008.

Risch, Barbara. "The Picture Changes: Stylistic Variation in Sitting Bull's Biographies." *Great Plains Quarterly* 20 (Fall 2000): 259–80.

Robinson, Doane. "The Rescue of Frances Kelly." *South Dakota Historical Collections* 4 (1908): 109–17.

Saum, Lewis O. "Stanley Huntley Interviews Sitting Bull: Event, Pseudo-Event or Fabrication?" *Montana: The Magazine of Western History* 32 (Spring 1982): 2–15.

Secoy, Frank Raymond. *Changing Military Patterns of the Great Plains Indians*. Reprint. Lincoln: University of Nebraska Press, 1992.

Sitting Bull College. https://www.sittingbull.edu/.

Smith, John Howard. *A Dream of the Judgment Day: American Millennialism and Apocalypticism, 1620–1890*. New York: Oxford University Press, 2021.

Smith, Sherry L. *The View from Officers' Row: Army Perceptions of Western Indians*. Tucson: University of Arizona Press, 1990.

Smoak, Gregory E. *Ghost Dances and Identity: Prophetic Religion and American Indian Ethnogenesis in the Nineteenth Century*. Berkeley: University of California Press, 2006.

Standing Bear, Luther. *Land of the Spotted Eagle*. Reprint. Lincoln: University of Nebraska Press, 1978.

Standing Bear, Luther. *My People the Sioux*. Reprint. Lincoln: University of Nebraska Press, 1975.

Stillman, Deanne. *Blood Brothers: The Story of the Strange Friendship between Sitting Bull and Buffalo Bill*. New York: Simon & Schuster, 2017.

Stirling, Mathew. *Three Pictographic Autobiographies of Sitting Bull*. Smithsonian Miscellaneous Collections, vol. 97, no. 5. Washington DC: Smithsonian Institution, 1938.

Szabo, Joyce M. "Mapped Battles and Visual Narratives: The Arrest and Killing of Sitting Bull." *American Indian Art Magazine*, Fall 1996.

Tatanka Iyotake (Sitting Bull). "Buffalo Robe," circa 1877–1881. Pigment on American bison hide. State Historical Society of North Dakota.

Trobriand, Phillipe Regis de. *Military Life in Dakota: The Journal of Philippe Regis de Trobriand*. Translated and edited by Lucile M. Kane. St. Paul, MN: Alvord Memorial Commission, 1951.

Turner, C. Frank. *Across the Medicine Line: The Epic Confrontation Between Sitting Bull and the North-West Mounted Police*. Toronto: McClelland and Stewart, 1973.

Turner, John Peter. *The North-West Mounted Police, 1873–1893*. Vol. 1. Ottawa: King's Printer and Controller of Stationery, 1950.

Üngör, Ugur Ümit. *Paramilitarism: Mass Violence in the Shadow of the State*. New York: Oxford University Press, 2020.

United States v. Sioux Nation of Indians, 448 U.S. 371, 1980. Retrieved from U.S. Supreme Court at https://supreme.justia.com/cases/federal/us/448/371/#376.

Utley, Robert M. *The Lance and the Shield: The Life and Times of Sitting Bull*. New York: Henry Holt, 1993.

Utley, Robert M. *The Last Days of the Sioux Nation*. New Haven, CT: Yale University Press, 1963.

Utley, Robert M. *The Last Sovereigns: Sitting Bull and the Resistance of the Free Lakota*. Lincoln: University of Nebraska Press, 2020.

van den Broeck, Karl. "Everything We Know About Sitting Bull's Crucifix Is Wrong." *True West Magazine*, October 29, 2018. https://truewestmagazine.com/article/everything-we-know-about-sitting-bulls-crucifix-is-wrong/.

Vestal, Stanley. *New Sources of Indian History*. Norman: University of Oklahoma Press, 1934.

Vestal, Stanley. *Sitting Bull: Champion of the Sioux*. 2nd ed. Norman: University of Oklahoma Press, 1957.

Vestal, Stanley. "Sitting Bull's Maiden Speech." *The Frontier, Magazine of the Northwest* 12 (March 1932): 269–71.

Vestal, Stanley. *Warpath: The True Story of the Fighting Sioux Told in a Biography of Chief White Bull*. Reprint. Lincoln: University of Nebraska Press, 1984.

Vestal, Stanley. "The Works of Sitting Bull: Real and Imaginary." *Southwest Review* 19 (April 1934): 265–78.

Waggoner, Josephine. *Witness: A Húŋkpapȟa Historian's Strong-Heart Song of the Lakotas*. Edited by Emily Levine. Lincoln: University of Nebraska Press, 2013.

Walker, James R. *Lakota Belief and Ritual*. Edited by Raymond J. DeMallie and Elaine A. Jahner. Lincoln: University of Nebraska Press, 1991.

Walker, James R. *Lakota Myth*. Edited by Elaine A. Jahner. Lincoln: University of Nebraska Press, 1983.

Walker, James R. *Lakota Society*. Edited by Raymond DeMallie. Lincoln: University of Nebraska Press, 1982.

Walker, Judson Elliott. *Campaigns of General Custer in the NorthWest and the Final Surrender of Sitting Bull*. New York: Jenkins & Thomas, 1881.

Warren, G. K., and Engineer Department, United States Army. *Preliminary Report of Explorations in Nebraska and Dakota, in the Years 1855–'56–'57*. Reprint. Washington DC: Government Printing Office, 1875.

Warren, Louis S. *God's Red Son: The Ghost Dance Religion and the Making of Modern America*. New York: Basic Books, 2017.

White, Richard. "The Winning of the West: The Expansion of the Western Sioux in the Eighteenth and Nineteenth Centuries." *Journal of American History* 65 (September 1978): 319–43.

Wilkins, David E. *American Indian Sovereignty and the U.S. Supreme Court: The Masking of Justice*. Austin: University of Texas Press, 2010.

Wishart, David J. *The Fur Trade of the American West: A Geographical Synthesis*. Lincoln: University of Nebraska Press, 1992.

Wong, Hertha Dawn. *Sending My Heart Back Across the Years: Tradition and Innovation in Native American Autobiography*. New York: Oxford University Press, 1992.

Wooster, Robert. *Nelson A. Miles and the Twilight of the Frontier Army*. Lincoln: University of Nebraska Press, 1993.

Yenne, Bill. *Sitting Bull*. Yardley, PA: Westholme Publishing, 2009.

Image Credits

1. Winter Count, twentieth century, Lakȟóta. Minneapolis Institute of Art, Gift of the Weiser Family Foundation. Used by permission.
2. Map, Treaty of Fort Laramie, 1851. North Dakota Studies Official State Website (https://www.ndstudies.gov/gr8/content/unit-iii-waves-development-1861-1920/lesson-1-changing-landscapes/topic-4-reservation-boundaries/section-6-standing-rock-reservation). Used by permission of the North Dakota Department of Public Instruction and the North Dakota State Historical Society.
3. Map, Treaty of Fort Laramie, 1868. North Dakota Studies Official State Website (https://www.ndstudies.gov/gr8/content/unit-iii-waves-development-1861-1920/lesson-1-changing-landscapes/topic-4-reservation-boundaries/section-6-standing-rock-reservation). Used by permission of the North Dakota Department of Public Instruction and the North Dakota State Historical Society.
4. Custer's War, c. 1900, Tȟatȟáŋka Waŋžíla (Henry Oscar One Bull). Minneapolis Institute of Art, The Christina N. and Swan J. Turnblad Memorial Fund. Used by permission.
5. Front Page, *Harper's Weekly*, December 8, 1877. Harper & Brothers, New York City (https://commons.wikimedia.org/wiki/File:Harpers_weekly_sitting_bull_8december1877.jpg), "Harpers weekly sitting bull 8december1877 [sic]," marked as public domain; more details on Wikimedia Commons: https://commons.wikimedia.org/wiki/Template:PD-1923.
6. Sitting Bull, half-length portrait, seated, facing front, holding calumet, 1881. Library of Congress.
7. Sitting Bull and Buffalo Bill. Library of Congress.
8. Lakota Reservation map prepared by Beehive Cartographers, Inc.
9. "Let us put our minds together and see what life we will make for our children." Yanker poster collection, Library of Congress.

10. MS 1929-a, drawing of war deeds of Sitting Bull and Jumping Bull, National Anthropological Archives, Smithsonian Institution. Used by permission.
11. In battle with Flatheads. MS 1929-b, Sitting Bull pictographic autobiography and related material, 1882–1923, National Anthropological Archives, Smithsonian Institution. Used by permission.
12. A Map Partly Suggested and Corrected by Sitting Bull, *New York Herald*, November 16, 1877.
13. In battle with Crow scouts accompanying General Nelson A. Miles. MS 1929-b, Sitting Bull pictographic autobiography and related material, 1882–1923, National Anthropological Archives, Smithsonian Institution. Used by permission.
14. Photograph of Buffalo Robe Painting by Sitting Bull. MacKenzie Art Gallery; Tatanka Iyotake (Sitting Bull), "Buffalo Robe," circa 1877–1881, pigment on American bison hide, State Historical Society of North Dakota, #10117. Used by permission.
15. US commissioners and delegations of Sioux chiefs visiting Washington, October 13, 1888. Library of Congress.

INDEX

Abenaki, 152–53
Allen, Alveren, 23–24, 132
Allison, Edward, 106, 113
Allison, William, 72
Andrews, George, 116
Arapaho, 13–16, 73–80
Arikara, 2, 13, 73, 138
Arthur, Chester A., 115
Assiniboine, 2, 4, 57, 98, 100

Baker, Eugene M., 10–11
Battle of Arrow Creek, 10–11
Battle of the Little Bighorn [Greasy Grass], 13–14, 26, 33, 35–36, 73–82, 98, 133–34
Battle of Killdeer Mountain, 6–7
Battle of Milk River, 19, 100–101
Battle of the Rosebud, 12–13, 73
Battle of Wolf Mountain, 16
Bear's Rib, 53
Benteen, Frederick W., 81–82
Big Foot [Spotted Elk], 32
bison herds, 1–3, 5, 7, 10, 18–19, 27, 33, 41–45, 60, 76–77, 83–87, 97, 102
Black Bird, 138, 146
Blackfeet, 2, 109
Black Hills [Paha Sapa], 5–7, 11, 16, 30, 33, 53–54, 58–59, 61, 68–73, 83–88, 93, 98, 124–25, 134, 144
Black Moon, 4, 23
Bone Tomahawk, 106
Bourke, Gregory, 3
Bozeman Trail, 7, 58
Brings Plenty, 55
Brotherton, David H., 104–5
Brown Shawl Woman, 2

Bruguier, John [Big Leggings], 85–86
Buisson, Marie Louise, 123
Bull Ghost, 28, 146
Bull Head, 31, 143, 146

Campbell, Walter S. [Stanley Vestal], 36–37, 53, 86, 138
Carlin, W. P., 83
Carlisle Indian Industrial School, 24, 132
Catches the Bear, 138
Cheyenne, 13–16, 58, 70, 73–80, 100
Chouteau Company, 6
Cleveland, Grover, 24, 136
Cody, William F., 24, 30, 133–36
Collins, Mary C., 28–29
Cowen, Benjamin R., 67
Crawler, 55
Crazy Horse, 13, 17, 60, 72, 111
Cree, 110
Creelman, James, 113
Cronau, Rudolf, 20, 115
Crook, George, 11, 13, 15–16, 72, 143–45
Crow, 2–4, 8, 13, 19, 24, 61–62, 67, 71, 73, 95, 100–101, 138
Crow Eagle, 132
Crow Foot, 4, 20, 31, 104
Crow King, 104, 106, 109
Culbertson, Fanny, 109
Custer, George Armstrong, 13–15, 35–36, 74–83, 98, 109, 134, 153

Dakota War, 6
Dawes, Henry L., 24, 123, 140

187

de Keredern de Trobriand, Philippe Régis Denis, 56
Densmore, Frances, 41
De Smet, Pierre-Jean, 58–59
Drum, William F., 30–31, 146

Eagle Chasing, Sam, 86
Eastman, Charles A., 68
Edmunds, Newton, 121–22
ethnic cleansing, 32–33

Fechet, Edmund G., 31
Flathead, 2–4, 65–66
Fletcher, Alice, 20
Fly, Joseph, 61–62
Flying By, 132
Fort Laramie treaties, 6–8, 11, 14, 16, 53, 58, 68–69, 72, 144
Four Horns, 3–4, 9, 23, 51, 60, 106–7
Four Robes, 4, 31, 135
Fox, Andrew, 146
fur trade, 6, 56

Gall, 13, 23, 58, 104, 106, 108–9, 138
Galpin, Charles, 58
Garfield, James A., 20, 110
Ghost Dance movement, 26–30, 32, 145–47
Gibbon, John, 11
Gilbert, Charles C., 111
Goff, Orlando S., 106
gold mining, 11, 53, 70, 72, 98, 134
Good Feather Woman, 2, 36
Grant, Ulysses S., 8–9, 11, 16, 72–73
Grass, John [Charging Bear], 23, 138, 140–41
Gray Eagle, 22, 128, 132
Gray Eagle, Clarence, 33
Great American Desert, 7
Great Sioux War, 11–16, 19, 20, 37, 70–88
Gros Ventre, 2, 110, 138

Grouard, Frank [Standing Bear; Grabber], 10, 57

Halsey, William, 133
Harney, William S., 54
Harrison, Benjamin, 29–30
Hayes, Rutherford B., 17, 93
Hedderich, Gus M., 100, 102
Her Holy Door, 2, 4, 7, 46, 57
Hidatsa, 2
Higheagle, Robert P., 41
His Horse Looking, 10
Holy Medicine, 32
Hunkpapa, 1, 4, 7, 9, 13, 23, 26, 46, 53–58, 60, 70, 74, 80, 83, 95, 121, 138, 143
Hungry Crow, 138
Hunt, Jerome, 128
Huntley, Stanley, 97–99

Iktomi, 5, 144

Jay Cooke and Company, 11
Johnson, Willis Fletcher, 36
Jumping Bull [Sitting Bull], 2–4, 107, 133

Kelly, Fanny, 7, 55
Kicking Bear, 27–29, 145
Kimball, James, 51
Kiowa, 2

Lakota [Teton], 1–38, 41–62, 65–88, 91–118, 123–47
LaPointe, Ernie, 37
Larpenteur, Charles, 56
Legaré, Jean Louis, 104–5
Light Hair, 4
Lincoln, Robert T., 116, 121
Little Assiniboine [*Hohe*; Jumping Bull], 4, 52, 57, 128
Logan, John A., 123

Index

Lone Man, John, 41, 143
Long Dog, 97, 132
Looks-for-Him-in-a-Tent, 3–4, 107
Low Dog, 108

Macdonell, Alexander, 105
Macleod, James F., 93
Magpie, 19, 100
Makes Room, 36
Mandan, 2, 138
Man That Smells His Hand, 83
Many Horses, 4, 104, 106, 109
Manypenny, George W., 16
Marsh, Grant, 121
Marty, Martin, 91–92, 124
McLaughlin, James, 23–24, 26, 28–29, 31, 121, 123, 136, 138, 143, 145–47
Métis, 10, 93, 102
Miles, Nelson A., 16, 19, 30, 32, 86–87, 100–101, 146
Miniconjou, 1, 27, 36, 70, 77–80, 83, 95, 138, 145
Mohawk, 152
Morgan, Thomas Jefferson, 145
Murray, William Henry Harrison, 151–54

National Indian Defense Association, 26
Nez Percé, 19, 95
Noble, John W., 30
North-West Mounted Police [Mounties], 17–19, 76, 91, 93

Oakley, Annie, 24, 133
Očhéthi Šakówiŋ, 1, 32, 60, 116
Oglala, 1, 7, 13, 17, 24, 55, 58, 60, 70, 80, 83, 132
Omaha, 2
One Bull, Henry Oscar, 4, 14–15, 23, 29, 36, 53, 73, 97, 106, 128, 130

Otis, Elwell S., 85
Otoe, 2

Paiute, 27, 145
Pass Beyond, 138
Pawnee, 2
Ponca, 2
Pratt, Daniel L., 20
Pratt, Richard Henry, 140, 141
Primeau, Louis, 145

Quimby, Horace, 22

Red Cloud, 7, 9, 30, 58, 68, 72, 118
Red Tomahawk, 31
Red Whirlwind, 29
Reno, Marcus A., 77, 81
reservation system, 7–11, 16, 19, 22, 24–30, 33, 60, 70–73, 83, 91, 105, 109, 121–25, 136, 140, 146, 151
Richaud, Louis, 72
Running Antelope, 106–8
Running Bull, 116

Salsbury, Nate, 136–37
Sans Arc, 1, 70, 83
Scarlet Woman, 4
Selwyn, William T., 111–12
Shannon, Peter C., 121–22
Sheridan, Philip H., 11–12, 14, 136
Short Bull, 29
Shoshone, 2
Sicangu [Brulé], 1, 20, 24, 30, 83, 117–18, 140
Sihasapa [Blackfoot], 1, 23
Sitting Bull [Jumping Badger, Hunkesni, Sacred Standshot], 1–38, 41–62, 65–88, 91–118, 123–47, 151–54
Smith, John C., 20, 22, 65
Snow on Hair, 4

Spotted-Horn-Bull, 146
Spotted Tail, 20, 30, 112, 118
Standing Bear, Luther, 24, 132
Standing Holy, 4, 23
Stanley, David S., 10
Stillson, Jerome B., 46, 76
Strike Kettle, 138
Sully, Alfred, 56
sun dance, 5, 12–13, 23, 24, 28, 70, 73, 102, 138
Swain, Peter T., 121–22

Tear, Wallace, 20, 22, 65, 67
Teller, Henry M., 121
Teller, James, 121–22
Terry, Alfred H., 11, 13–14, 17, 74, 93–94, 125, 131
thunderbird, 3, 49
Thunder Hawks, 106
Tibbles, Thomas H., 20
transcontinental railroads, 8, 10, 68, 130
Twin Woman, 2
Two Kettle, 1

Utley, Robert M., 37

Vilas, William F., 140

Walking Elk, 116
Walks Looking, 23, 146
Wakantanka, 4–5, 12, 27, 41, 43–46, 48, 58–59, 60, 70–73, 81, 83, 86, 108, 111, 115, 121, 146
Walsh, James M., 17, 19, 76, 91, 95, 105
Warren, Gouverneur K., 53
Weldon, Catherine [Caroline Schlatter], 26
Wells, Phillip, 121
White, E. D., 128
White Bird, 95
White Buffalo Calf Maiden, 23, 41–45
White Bull, Joseph, 4, 11, 13, 36, 53, 86, 138
Williamson, John P., 20
winter counts, 1–2, 61
Wounded Knee massacre, 30, 32–33
Wovoka, 27–29, 145

Yanktonai, 105, 111, 116
Yellowstone National Park, 19